MW01673185

idea of ??a realistic utopia

Collin J. Anthony

ACKNOWLEDGEMENTS

First of all, I would like to thank my dissertation supervisor, Kok-Chor Tan, and my committee members, Samuel Freeman and Errol Lord, for their patience and helpful guidance throughout the years. Special thanks are also in order for Adrienne Martin for her openness and honesty about the various challenges of the dissertation process.

I must also express my sincerest gratitude to my dear friend, Govind Persad, for his mentorship and his friendly philosophical engagements. Sriram Sridharan, Karthik Sethuraman, Shirley Leung, Seth Shannin, Bezhou Feng, Eric Chen, Luke Reilly, and Chris Ceperley are also due thanks for their enduring friendship throughout my time in Kings Court English College House.

I must also thank my mother for her unwavering love and support throughout the course of my life.

Finally, I must thank Krimo Bokreta, Jorge Santiago-Aviles, Marta Rivas-Olmeda, Cam Grey, Ann Vernon-Grey, and the other members of the KCECH community for making Penn more than just a place of scholarly pursuits, but a place for social enrichment.

ABSTRACT

THE IDEA OF A REALISTIC UTOPIA

COLLIN ANTHONY

KOK-CHOR TAN

The purpose of this dissertation is to articulate the proper aims and limits of political philosophy by expanding upon John Rawls's idea of a realistic utopia and applying it to various debates in contemporary political philosophy. First, I defend the importance of ideal theory in constructing a theory of justice and respond to various critics, such as Amartya Sen and others, who argue that ideal theory is neither necessary nor sufficient for our work to advance justice in society. Second, I argue that empirical facts must be included in our reasoning about fundamental principles of justice, contrary to theorists such as G.A. Cohen who argues that political theorizing should proceed independently of such facts. Finally, I conclude with some reflecting thoughts on the importance of articulating a conception of justice that avoids hopelessly utopian ideals. In doing so, I defend the vision of a realistically utopian society as one that both answers our most fundamental interests and also provides us with the best chance of realizing justice in the world.

TABLE OF CONTENTS

PREFACE

This work in political philosophy explicates and defends Rawls's idea of a realistic utopia in order to respond to many debates that have arisen in the contemporary philosophical literature surrounding the nature of justice. These debates include: the relevance of utopianism and realism, the relationship between principles of justice and empirical facts, and the importance of ideal theory in constructing a conception of justice. Not surprisingly, new work is produced within these topics at a healthy pace and some of this material could not be fully explored in this dissertation. One work that is worthy of note is Gerald Gaus's book, *The Tyranny of the Ideal*, which was published after my chapter on ideal theory had already been drafted and completed.[1] As such, despite its importance, my dissertation does not directly address its main arguments, and only refers to it in a limited capacity . Nevertheless, many of the ideas advocated for here can be expanded upon and applied to his work, which I will leave for future research and exploration.

[1] Gaus, Gerald. *The Tyranny of the Ideal.* Princeton University Press, 2016.

Chapter 1: Three Dichotomies in Political Philosophy[2]

I. The Purpose of the Dissertation

The purpose of this dissertation is to explore three dichotomies that can be said to characterize several debates in political philosophy: realism vs. utopianism, ideal vs. nonideal theory, and fact-sensitivity vs. fact-insensitivity. Each of these dichotomies involves interrelated issues surrounding the methods of political philosophy, the nature of justice, and the proper goals and aspirations we should have when constructing a theory of justice. The claim that I defend is as follows: the **idea of a realistic utopia**—an important idea that appears in the work of John Rawls—is the most appropriate framework for resolving these three dichotomies and will yield important insights about the goals and methods of political philosophy. In developing the idea, I argue that Rawls's understanding of justice represents a position that (a) establishes the importance of **ideal theory**, (b) requires a **sensitivity to empirical facts**, and (c) provides a vision of society that is **utopian**, yet is still **realistically achievable**.

Before turning to our explication of these dichotomies, let me illustrate the importance of these questions with an example. Suppose a socialist egalitarian asserts that justice requires the complete equality of resources among all persons, and that we reply with the following: "Your conception of justice is unachievable—human beings will never be able to act in ways to sustain perfect equality of resources due to human

---

[2] All notes to Rawls's work after the first citation will follow this notation: *Theory of Justice* (TJ), *Political Liberalism* (PL), *Justice as Fairness* (JF), *The Law of Peoples*, (LP), "Kantian Constructivism," (KC), and *Collected Papers* (CP).

motivational limitations and imperfect human institutions. Consequently, your conception of justice must be false as it is clearly infeasible and incompatible with our human nature." Imagine that the socialist replies: "That is no objection to my theory at all, for I am not making any background assumptions about human behavior, psychology or social institutions. If we hold human psychology as an irrelevant variable, my theory is without flaw. Justice mandates perfect equality. If it turns out that human beings *are* hopelessly selfish, then so much the worse for humans. The content of justice is not undermined by our imperfect nature and our inability to realize it."

These exchanges are not uncommon in debates surrounding the demands of justice, and they highlight important issues about some sources of disagreement between different schools of thought. From this example, we can see that error, if there exists any, is much more likely to be the result of different underlying assumptions about what should and should not be taken for granted when theorizing about political philosophy in the first place, and not the result of logical flaws in conclusions drawn from the stated premises. For, it may very well be true that if human psychology were irrelevant, perfect equality should be our target. But is this really the most appropriate way to argue for this conclusion? Should we really ignore features about humans when reasoning about justice? Does it come at too high a cost, akin to a Pyrrhic victory? To answer these questions, we must investigate the methodology and background assumptions about political philosophy itself. Upon doing so, we may find that how we answer these more fundamental questions shapes the principles we select as candidates for how best to live in society with one another.

From our initial example between the socialist and her critic, we can expand upon it and parse out the multiple dichotomies where disagreements lie with respect to these more basic methodological questions about political theorizing. They can be characterized in the following ways:

(a) Ideal and Nonideal Theory

One such dichotomy we can use to characterize these disagreements is between ideal and nonideal theory. [3] For instance, we may choose to characterize the socialist as utilizing ideal theory to make her claim that perfect equality is required. But what does it mean to say "ideal" theory? One way to describe it is to say that ideal theory is a method of theorizing that "idealizes" away certain variables—such as human psychology—to either emphasize a normative point, or to simplify our reasoning about justice. The general motivation to do so would be that the social world and human behavior are too complex to evaluate all at once, and that the best tactic would be to isolate features by holding others constant so that we can pinpoint something of normative importance.

We are already used to this kind of tool in the empirical sciences—that is, we ignore friction in physics, or we assume the perfect competition of markets in

[3] For an alternative account for how to capture the distinction between ideal and nonideal theory, see Valentini, Laura. "Ideal and Nonideal Theory: A Conceptual Map." *Philosophy Compass* 17 (2009): 332-55, and Hamlin, Alan and Zofia Stemplowska. "Theory, Ideal Theory, and the Theory of Ideals." *Political Studies Review* 10 (2012): 48-62.

economics. We know that variables such as friction matter, but in order to make headway in determining more fundamental principles, we need to idealize away from them and then slowly add these variables in later as we come to better grasp the scientific principles at stake more clearly.[4]

Similarly, some uses of ideal theory in political philosophy can be said to mirror some of these tactics. We have already seen in our initial example how some egalitarians may choose to ignore features of human psychology when arguing for their claims. Other instances can be described as well. For example, in global justice, some theorists may choose to ignore the existence of borders when theorizing about the best principle to govern the distribution of resources in the world. For these theorists, it is not that they completely disregard the importance of borders—just like physicists know that friction is important—it is rather that *borders are not morally relevant for deciding fundamental principles.*[5] For these theorists, the existence of borders only confounds our thinking about justice; it is best if we ignore them and settle the fundamental principles of justice first before can we consider other variables, such as borders. As this

---

[4] Some philosophers of science argue for the distinction between "abstraction" on the one hand and "idealization" on the other. The central idea is that abstraction ignores a feature of the world, whereas idealization assumes something that is *false* in order to simplify the world. For example, a physicist may abstract from friction (since it is subtracted away from the world), and an economist may idealize a market (perfect competition is false as it does not exist). See Cartwright, Nancy. *How the Laws of Physics Lie.* Oxford University Press, 1983. For a further discussion of this distinction see Weisberg, Michael. "Three Kinds of Idealization," *The Journal of Philosophy* 104, no. 12 (2007): 639-659. Also, to see how abstraction and idealization relates to ethics, see O'Neill, Onora. *Towards Justice and Virtue: A Constructivist Account of Practical Reasoning.* Cambridge University Press, 1996: 40-45. Also see Gaus, Gerald. *The Tyranny of the Ideal.* Princeton University Press, 2016: 36-38.

[5] For an example of this kind of theorizing, see Beitz, Charles. "Justice and International Relations," *Philosophy and Public Affairs* 4, no. 4 (1975): 376. He argues that "we should not view national boundaries as having fundamental moral significance," and seeks to apply a principle of redistribution to the entire globe.

example illustrates, we can better see how theorists "idealize" away certain features of the world in order to theorize more fruitfully about principles by removing some of the complexity involved.

Of course, the method of ideal theory—understood in this way—is not without challenges. Many critics have voiced concerns about the danger of idealizing away central features of the world—such as borders—or of human capacities. While these critics are typically labeled as proponents of "nonideal" theory, it is a bit of a misnomer to do so. For what bothers many critics of ideal theory is *not the engagement in idealization per se*, but *the variables being idealized away themselves*. For instance, a common objection to the global theorist who ignores the existence of borders is to say that borders *are* relevant at the fundamental level and should never be idealized away.[6] The objection is not that *no* idealization can ever occur. Even the harshest critic of ideal theory would agree that it is acceptable to ignore *some* features of the world. For instance, few would object to the idealizing away of individual differences about tastes and preferences, or of the variation of individual personality traits.[7] Moreover, we can do so without denying the normative importance that some of those features may eventually have further downstream in our moral framework. In other words, such features would simply operate at a later stage—similar to how friction may be added

[6] Many theorists hold that borders matter for they define a normatively salient set of associations and relationships that exist among the members within the borders. See, for instance, Scheffler, Samuel. *Boundaries and Allegiances*. Oxford University Press, 2002.

[7] We may acknowledge that there *are* individual differences, but we can idealize away from the *specific sets of preferences*—such as the preference for vanilla ice cream over chocolate.

back into our consideration at a later point of our investigation after we have uncovered a more fundamental principle of physics.

Consequently, when we describe a "nonideal" theorist, we should envision one who is highly critical of idealizing away a certain *set* of variables, namely ones that have been commonly discussed in the literature—features such as human selfishness, the workings of social institutions, the existence of borders, or the assumption of full compliance, to name a few. Such theorists remind us to be extremely cautious when engaging in idealization and exhort us to be certain that we have adequate justification for ignoring certain features of ourselves and the world when theorizing about justice.

(b) Realism and Utopianism

Another dichotomy that can be described in debates surrounding the constraints and methods of political theorizing is the distinction between realism and utopianism.[8] Some interpret the task of political philosophy to mean that we should strive to describe the principles that would govern a utopia that is the *best of all possible worlds.* In this sense, one might imagine that our theoretical task would be to "start from scratch" in the building of our world, using whatever normative guidance and reasoning we have in order to determine what kind of life we should live and what kind of beings we should become.[9] There would be, in a sense, no limits at all to our inquiry, with the exception of perhaps our capacity for imagination and of our rationality and moral intuitions.

---

[8] The literature sometimes describes this dichotomy as part of the ideal/non-ideal distinction. See Valentini (2009). However, for clarification purposes, I wish to distinguish them.

[9] Rawls describes Leibnitz's philosophy as falling into this category: "Another idea is that of moral philosophy as importantly a study of the ethics of creation, that is, of the principles of good and evil and

Since there are relatively few contemporary examples of this approach, a more modest account of this dichotomy should be articulated. According to this more limited approach, utopianism allows us to largely ignore concerns about *feasibility* and *achievability* when constructing a picture of what the perfect society is. For instance, G.A. Cohen argues that a socialist society is desirable and the best we can envision for ourselves, even though he concedes that he is agnostic about whether or not it is achievable.[10] For Cohen, feasibility is not a general constraint on our political principles, and the construction of the perfect utopian society is an exercise that is independent of the question of how to implement such a society in the actual world.

What value is there to such an approach? After all, if we cannot achieve the perfect society—on what basis can we argue for it? There are two replies we can offer here. First, Cohen could argue that it is a mistake to assume that *all* value lies in implementation, and that there is value to be attained in discerning the very idea of a utopian society as a purely rational feat. Mathematicians may rely upon similar justifications for their work when the possibility of applying any of it to the actual world may be limited.

However, a second way to defend the irrelevance of feasibility and achievability is to illustrate it with the Kantian idea of a *regulative ideal*. According to Kant, one of

---

of right and wrong that guide the divine will in the creation of the world." See Rawls, John. *Lectures on the History of Moral Philosophy*, ed. by Barbara Herman. Harvard University Press, 2000: 107.
[10] See Cohen, G.A. *Why not Socialism?* Princeton University Press, 2009. Also see Gilabert, Pablo. "Debate: Feasibility and Socialism," *The Journal of Political Philosophy* 19, no. 1 (2011): 52-63. And Gheaus, Anca. "The Feasibility Constraint on the Concept of Justice," *The Philosophical Quarterly* 63, no. 252 (2013): 445-464.

our duties is that of self-perfection. However, Kant believes that perfection is impossible for us to ever attain—it is instead "a rudder by which to steer oneself."[11] Kant states: "It is a human being's duty to strive for this perfection, but not to reach it . . . and his compliance with this duty can, accordingly consist only in continual progress."[12] Hence, a regulative ideal can be valuable irrespective of our ability to achieve it, for it can guide us toward correct actions and help us eradicate the ever-deceptive and ubiquitous motive of self-love.[13]

On this reading, utopian modes of thought—characterized by the irrelevance of feasibility or achievability—may allow us to construct perfect models that can direct the design of institutions in political philosophy, or guide our intentions in the domain of moral philosophy. So, while it may be impossible to ever reach a utopia, the model can still provide us with guidance when attempting to improve our current state of affairs. On this account, without such guidance, our reformations would be aimless and without a clear goal. Put simply, to improve the current state of affairs, one must have a blueprint to guide decision making.

Not surprisingly, realists object to these two strands of utopianism. With respect to the notion of "starting from scratch" and building the best possible world, realists resist the broad and limitless explorations into what society could be like. They assert that, while these musings may be appropriate as works of fiction within literature, they

---

[11] See Grenberg, Jeanine. *Kant and the Ethics of Humility: A Story of Dependence, Corruption and Virtue*. Cambridge University Press, 2005: 89.
[12] Kant, Immanuel. *The Metaphysics of Morals*, trans. and ed. by M.J. Gregor, in *The Cambridge Edition of the Works of Immanuel Kant*. Cambridge University Press, 1991: 446.
[13] For a more detailed account of this see, Grenberg (2005): 89-95.

cannot have much philosophical value with respect to how we should organize society. At best, they could perhaps expand our imagination by enabling us to envision alternate realities. But at worst, they can be dangerous fancies that lead us astray from what we can actually hope to achieve—forever tempting people with a vision that is impossible, leading to endless frustration and implacable resentment.[14] For this reason, realists also reject the idea that we should ignore concerns of feasibility and achievability in our theories of justice. They tend to appeal to the dictum that "ought implies can," and argue that, if the perfect society cannot actually be attainable, then the normative force of the utopian vision should be blunted.

In addition, other theorists argue that the fixation on determining what the perfect society is will not provide us with the necessary tools to make improvements in society. Amartya Sen, for example, has argued that constructing a utopia that is perfectly just is "neither necessary nor sufficient" in aiding us in our choice to improve the current state affairs.[15]

In light of these worries, realists tend to highlight the "here and now" and emphasize the limitations that current political structures or individual motivational patterns pose for any attempts at change to society. Consequently, realists will not devote much argumentative efforts in constructing the perfect or flawless society, but

---

[14] See Galston, William. "Realism in Political Theory," *European Journal of Political Theory* 9, no. 4 (2010): 385-411, for a discussion on this point.

[15] See Sen, Amartya. *The Idea of Justice*. Harvard University Press, 2009. Also, Sen, Amartya. "What do we want from a Theory of Justice?" *The Journal of Philosophy* 53, no. 5 (2006): 215-238.

rather highlight feasible improvements that we can make to society, given what we already know and whatever limitations are in place.[16]

(c) Fact-Sensitivity vs Fact-Insensitivity

The final dichotomy that I explore relates to two separate issues: first, whether or not our fundamental principles of justice are "fact-free" in the sense that they do not rely upon any facts to justify them, and second, whether or not it is permissible to allow any facts whatsoever into our justification of principles of justice. According to G.A. Cohen, for a principle of justice to be truly fundamental, it must lie at the summit of our normative convictions and cannot express any reliance upon facts.[17] If it does, as he believes Rawls's conception of justice does, we should be able to unearth a fundamental principle by probing for the ultimate justification for it that explains why those facts are relevant.

If we return to our example of the socialist and her critic, the socialist could be asserting a "fact-free" commitment to equality in the sense that she believes that there are no facts required to justify her stance—it is simply the most fundamental belief she has: "justice demands equality." We can test this by inquiring why she believes this. If she does not need to appeal to a fact to do so, she has reached the summit of her beliefs.

---

[16] See Wiens, David. "Prescribing Institutions without Ideal Theory," *The Journal of Political Philosophy* 20, no. 1 (2012): 45-70.
[17] Cohen, G.A. *Rescuing Justice and Equality*. Harvard University Press, 2008.

We can now turn to the second element of the dichotomy, according to which facts should have no bearing whatsoever in our justification of justice. The socialist, in defending her conception of equality, challenges her critic for invoking facts about human nature to counter her claim. Philosophers such as Cohen would argue that such a move is unwarranted, as such considerations are irrelevant to justice. Justice, on this account, is primarily a conceptual truth that is *applied* to factual circumstances. What justice requires, in other words, can never be challenged by factual circumstances.

Other philosophers, such as Rawls, deny this claim. They argue that facts must be at the forefront of our theorizing about justice. Otherwise, we are left with a conundrum as to how we should go about determining principles of justice that persons can agree upon. For, if we cannot rely upon facts, it is unclear that people we have enough information to figure out what justice requires.

In addition, Rawls believes that our reliance on facts makes justice applicable to us. If we ignore factual constraints, our resultant theory of justice will be distant and detached from our own conception of ourselves. As such, it could not serve the basis for a public criterion of justice that is capable of generating agreement.

II. Moving Forward

Having laid out the three dichotomies with respect to the methods and aims of political philosophy, I am now in a position to outline the chapters of my dissertation: In chapter 2, I briefly describe Rawls's idea of a realistic utopia, drawing upon textual support to provide a more detailed picture of his goals and methods for political philosophy. In chapter 3 and 4, I argue for the importance of ideal theory as defined by Rawls and defend it from various critics, including Amartya Sen who argue that it is neither necessary nor sufficient for advancing justice in the world. In chapter 5, I argue for the importance of empirical facts in our understanding of justice, and show that we cannot abstract away from all such facts when articulating the requirements of justice. And finally, in chapter 6, I conclude by highlighting how Rawls's methodology for determining principles of justice avoids hopelessly utopian ideals and argue for why Rawls's vision of a realistic utopia is the proper orientation of political philosophy.

Chapter 2: The Idea of a Realistic Utopia

> We view political philosophy as realistically utopian: that is, as probing the limits of practicable political possibility. Our hope for the future of our society rests on the belief that the social world allows at least a decent political order, so that a reasonably just, though not perfect, democratic regime is possible. So we ask: What would a just democratic society be like under reasonably favorable but still possible historical conditions, conditions allowed by the tendencies of the social world? What ideals and principles would such a society try to realize given the circumstances of justice in a democratic culture as we know them?[18]

I. Introduction

At first glance, the idea of a realistic utopia appears contradictory—what conceptual clarity could be gained by juxtaposing two seemingly incompatible notions together in a single idea? In order to answer this question, I must unpack the various components that inform Rawls's understanding of it.

Rawls first mentions the idea of a realistic utopia within the context of global justice in the *Law of Peoples*.[19] While the idea initially refers to the capacity for liberal and non-liberal decent societies to achieve lasting peace, Rawls himself extends the application of the idea to a conception of justice more generally in *Justice as Fairness*.[20] I will focus on that more general application here.

According to Rawls, inherent in the notion of a realistic utopia is a commitment to two governing judgments about what a conception of justice should do:

> (1) "Extend what are ordinarily thought to be the limits of practical political possibility;"[21] and

---

[18] Rawls, John. *Justice as Fairness*. Harvard University Press, 2001: 4.
[19] Rawls, John. *The Law of Peoples*. Harvard University Press, 1999.
[20] JF, 4-5, 13.
[21] LP, 11

> (2) "Depict an *achievable* social world....not a mere logical possibility, but one that connects with the deep tendencies and inclinations of the social world."[22]

Each of these judgments corresponds, respectively, to the utopian and realistic elements of justice. I will discuss each of these elements below.

(a) A Realistic *Utopia*

The first judgment gives voice to the utopian aspirations of a theory of justice. In society as we experience it, we are regularly reminded of the obstacles that limit the foreseeable possibilities of social progress, such as the memory of our historical failures, the perpetual conflicts of interest, and the feelings of political estrangement. Moreover, these obstacles tend to cement themselves into our normative attitudes towards the world, taking root in our considered judgments and coloring our view of what is ultimately possible for society. To provide an illustration, Rawls states, "there are long periods in the history of any society during which certain basic questions lead to deep and sharp conflict and it seems difficult if not impossible to find any reasoned common ground for political agreement."[23] Rawls cites the brutal conflict between Catholics and Protestants during the Reformation, the debates between the Federalists and the Anti-Federalists during the drafting of the American Constitution, and the perennial debates regarding the balance of liberty and equality in modern societies as examples that influence our pessimism about the possibility for genuine agreement about principles for a just society. From this history of disagreement, we may ultimately think that

[22] LP, 128.
[23] JF, 1.

justice can only be an endless power struggle between different competing and irreconcilable interests, with the only hope for agreement being a mere *modus vivendi*. Or, we may come to accept as part of the natural order the necessity of deep social inequalities with little recourse available to those who are worst off. As these illustrations show, the real danger, for Rawls, is that we may simply learn to respond to these intractable disputes by resigning ourselves to our existing situation, unable and unwilling to reach for the basis of a broader consensus or political agreement.

In the face of these pessimistic tendencies, a conception of justice must be, in part, utopian; it must expand our worldview and enable us to imagine new possibilities for society that have been deemed infeasible by our hardened hearts through our daily confrontations with the world. As Rawls states, "the limits of the possible are not given by the actual," and it is therefore up to us to construct a framework for justice that extends beyond the actual by showing how social and political institutions may be arranged differently, giving rise to a new political reality that is more just than the current state of affairs.[24] Without these aspirational elements of justice, we will perpetually be constrained by our actual circumstances and doomed to replicate our frustrations and disappointments without any reasonable hope for improvement.

Described in this way, a theory of justice should be, in a sense, expansive and broadening. It must give us reason to hope for an alternative arrangement of society that seeks to better respond to our fundamental interests as citizens.

---

[24] LP, 12.

(b) A *Realistic* Utopia

The second governing judgment reflects the realistic dimensions of justice. It urges us to temper our aspirations and ground them in the realities of human nature and the circumstances of society which pose limitations on what we can strive to achieve. As Rawls insists, we are not interested in mere "logical possibilities" of perfectly just societies, but rather genuine options that can reliably connect with the general capacities of human beings and the indelible features that characterize liberal democratic societies.

The reason for this is because we want to ensure that we have principles of justice "that we can understand and act on, approve, and endorse."[25] If our conception of justice fails to connect with our fundamental interests and our capacities, there is little assurance that humans will reliably act upon it over time. In this sense, an important realistic thread of Rawls's work is the importance of *stability* in our political theories. It is of no use to us to produce a picture of the perfect society that can only have momentary success amidst very specific circumstances. Instead, we require a society that answers to the general features of social life and of our psychological capacities. It is only then will a stable and just society be possible for us.

Failure to internalize these realistic elements will yield conceptions of justice that are inapplicable and even harmful to human societies. Let us illustrate with an example from Hume:

---

[25] LP, 7.

> We shall suppose, that a creature, possessed of reason, but unacquainted with human nature, deliberates with himself what RULES of justice or property would best promote public interest, and establish peace and security among mankind: His most obvious thought would be, *to assign the largest possessions to the most extensive virtue*, and give every one the power of doing good, proportioned to his inclination. In a perfect theocracy, where a being, infinitely intelligent, governs by particular volitions, this rule would certainly have place, and might serve to the wisest purposes: But were mankind to execute such a law; so great is the uncertainty of merit, both from its natural obscurity, and from the self-conceit of each individual, that no determinate rule of conduct would ever result from it; and the total dissolution of society must be the immediate consequence....*A rule, which, in speculation, may seem the most advantageous to society, may yet be found, in practice, totally pernicious and destructive.*[26]

From this passage, we can see that Hume issues a serious warning to utopian modes of reasoning; if we were to speculate, while being "unacquainted with human nature," or without regard to the effects of that rule on society, we would produce a "destructive" result. In Hume's example, if we ignore the limitations of human knowledge—if we do not acknowledge that we are not infinitely intelligent and are sometimes unaware of our own intentions, let alone the intentions of others—there would be no way to determine how to employ the rule "to each according to his virtue" without devolving into muddled and limited speculations. As a result, it should be eliminated as a possibility for a principle of justice. Hume ends his discussion by saying: "We may conclude, therefore, that, in order to establish laws for the regulation of property, we must be acquainted with the nature and situation of man."[27]

---

[26] Hume, David. *Enquiry Concerning Principle of Morals*, Section III, "Of Justice," Part II. https://www.gutenberg.org/files/4320/4320-h/4320-h.htm#2H_SECT3 (2010, January 12th).
[27] Ibid.

Rawls echoes Hume's conclusions here by quoting Rousseau, who famously claims that we must "take men as they are" when devising principles of justice.[28] Rawls interprets this to mean that we must be aware of the limitations that human nature imposes upon us and that we must employ "workable" principles of justice.[29] "Workable" for Rawls means that they must be *public* conceptions of justice that are "openly observable" and amenable to "interpersonal comparisons" in society.[30] The principle, "to each according to one's virtue," would fail this test for, as Hume points out, there is no easily accessible method by which public institutions could determine each person's level of virtue and the requisite reward for it.[31]

So far then, the realistic elements of justice emphasize the following: (1) human nature, (2) the general circumstances of society, (3) stability, and (4) workability. Of course, significant debate lies in the much harder question regarding *which* features of human nature and of society are important, and how these relate to stability and workability. I will discuss these in greater detail in later chapters.

(c) A *Realistic Utopia*

So, how does Rawls combine these two different goals into one coherent vision? According to Rawls, there are several features that a realistic utopia as a whole must

---

[28] LP, 13. For the reference to Rousseau's injunction, see Rousseau, Jean-Jacques. *The Social Contract*, in *Classics of Political and Moral Philosophy*, 2nd edition, ed. by Steven Cahn. Oxford University Press, 2012: 561.

[29] LP, 13.

[30] Ibid., 13.

[31] Rawls himself argues that the principle of utility and the capability approach to justice would similarly fail as workable public conceptions of justice. See Rawls, John. *Political Liberalism*. Columbia University Press, 1993: 13 for this argument.

contain if it is to be an appropriate conception of justice. First, a theory of justice must "use political (moral ideals), principles and concepts to specify a reasonable and just society."[32] While this may sound broad and more utopian in spirit, Rawls insists that these ideals must be completely contained "within the category of the political."[33] What Rawls means is that the conception of society and of the concepts employed to articulate a conception of justice must be "available in the public political culture of a liberal constitutional regime" and "not [from] any comprehensive doctrine, which always extends beyond the category of the political."[34] In other words, the notion of, say, freedom and equality employed by many conceptions of justice cannot be understood *solely* from within a singular religious worldview or from a comprehensive philosophical doctrine about the nature of free will. Instead, the freedom and equality of persons must be available in the language, structure and shared history of democratic institutions that citizens employ openly to one another. In doing so, there is greater scope for agreement and consensus on principles of justice that are based on shared normative concepts that are available and accessible to all citizens.

Other political norms that Rawls includes—in addition to the freedom and equality of citizens—is a set of political virtues such as the desire for "cooperation," "a sense of fairness," "tolerance," and "a willingness to meet others half-way."[35] These guiding norms do not require us to appeal to a unique moral doctrine for their ultimate

---

[32] LP, 14.
[33] LP, 15.
[34] LP, 15.
[35] LP, 15.

justification—they can be supported from a multitude of different conceptions of the good—and they can be assumed as a "given" within society in which people accept that social cooperation for mutual benefit is its defining feature.[36] If we define society in any other way—say, as the joint endeavor to ensure the salvation of souls, or as a cooperative effort to produce perfect selfless individuals—our political ideals and virtues will extend into objectionable utopian standards that will unlikely yield agreement or attain stability over time.

One important political norm to highlight on its own is that of reciprocity. According to Rawls:

> This criterion [of reciprocity] requires that, when terms are proposed...those proposing them must think it at least reasonable for others to accept them, as free and equal citizens, and not as dominated or manipulated or under pressure caused by an inferior political or social position.[37]

In this sense, reciprocity works with other political norms to establish a standpoint of justice that transcends current political and social realities in which vast inequalities may generate an unequal bargaining position between citizens. No conception of justice can be formulated if citizens cannot deliberate within a fair and reasonable standpoint from which citizens may decide upon principles of justice. Otherwise, any agreements would be unstable compromises, easily undermined by shifts in power or changes in interests. The norm of reciprocity ensures that any agreement that is reached after deliberation is agreed to *for the right reasons*—not out of fear, intimidation or unfair bargaining

[36] For a broader discussion of Rawls's "overlapping consensus," see PL, 133-172.
[37] LP, 14.

positions. In other words, it imposes a limit on the circumstances under which deliberation may take place that all parties should be able to accept as fair and reasonable. Such agreements will then be stable and at low risk of being undermined by changes in circumstances.

The norm of reciprocity is in this sense utopian, for it requires that citizens move beyond their current interests and think normatively within a standpoint that answers to our more fundamental interests as citizens: the ability to freely pursue a conception of the good, and to develop a sense of justice—or what Rawls calls the "two moral powers."[38]

And yet, at the same time, the criterion of reciprocity is realistic. Rawls is not demanding that we cultivate a capacity that we do not have, or one that is unreliable and limited. A concern for reciprocity, unlike say beneficence or altruism, is a reliable and stable human capacity that can be said to be at the heart of relations within a political society. In Part III of a *Theory of Justice*, Rawls even develops an account which establishes how "reciprocity is the fundamental psychological mechanism implicated in the development of moral motivation" and that, because of this, principles based upon reciprocity would "develop naturally out of preexisting psychological materials."[39] By grounding the source of basic political norms in fundamental human psychology, Rawls believes that accepting his conception of justice will not be an insurmountable task

---

[38] PL, 19.

[39] Scheffler, Samuel. "Rawls and Utilitarianism," in *The Cambridge Companion to Rawls,* Cambridge University Press, 2002: 435. Also see Rawls, John. *A Theory of Justice*. Harvard University Press, 1999: 433 where Rawls describes reciprocity as a "deep psychological fact," without which "our nature would be very different and fruitful social cooperation fragile if not impossible."

capable of only saints or the chosen few. It will be available to all, and will answer to citizens' deepest psychological tendencies, thereby ensuring stability and reliable acceptance over time.[40]

By limiting our normative ideals to political concepts within the scope of human psychology and within the culture of democratic institutions, we can maintain the vision of a realistic utopia without contradiction. A conception of justice is utopian in that it can expand the possibilities of social organization by appealing to normative goals that can be utilized to critically examine current social institutions. Yet, at the same time, this critical standpoint will be realistically grounded in what citizens *qua* citizens are already capable of accepting as it is compatible with their deepest psychology, their fundamental interests, as well as with the commitments within their social and political culture.

A final feature of a realistic utopia is that there must be an acknowledgement and acceptance of the fact of reasonable pluralism.[41] The fact of reasonable pluralism is the fact that citizens will naturally arrive at differing conclusions about fundamental values in life through the free use of their reason. The explanation for this is that citizens are constrained by imperfect information and limited capacities to weigh and evaluate evidence, or what Rawls calls "the burdens of judgment."[42] In other words, it

---

[40] Rawls contrasts this approach with that of the demands of utilitarianism, which requires that all citizens develop an expansive sympathy for all, and demands that the worst off members act the for the sake of those more fortunate when aggregate utility would be increased. For Rawls, this is unacceptable and will not reliably develop and persist as part of the normal course of moral development. See TJ, 437.
[41] JF, 4.
[42] JF, 35.

is unreasonable to expect citizens to converge on a particular conception of the good given the immense diversity of experiences and the differing responses to these experiences available to citizens. On Rawls's view then, the fact of reasonable pluralism must then be "permanent as it persists indefinitely under free democratic institutions."[43]

Given the indelible fact of reasonable pluralism, we would not do well in employing a principle of justice that ignored it—say, by instituting a principle of justice that required the unanimous agreement upon a comprehensive religious or philosophical doctrine. Doing so would disrupt the stability of a conception of justice and would not garner reliable adherence to it, as the state would have to resort to coercive tactics to enforce agreement. Citizens who would endure such policies would garner resentment and hatred for the state, awaiting the chance to overthrow it and replace it. This kind of inevitable vying for power would threaten to undermine and delegitimize the governing institutions in society. As a result, persons would reject any comprehensive doctrines as suitable claims for political organization, and would assert the importance of reasonable pluralism as a guiding feature of society. Otherwise, stability would not be realistically achievable, and persons would not be assured that their fundamental interests could be adequately safeguarded.

---

[43] JF, 4.

Given these considerations, Rawls states that "this fact of reasonable pluralism limits what is practicably possible."[44] While it may be an interesting philosophical exercise to provide a hypothetical picture of the perfectly just society that existed in a world in which humans were omniscient and did not suffer from the burdens of judgement—perhaps yielding a society in which everyone agreed upon a unique conception of the good—this would not be an acceptable guide for what justice actually requires of us. The mere fact that we could theoretically perform *that* exercise would be irrelevant and utopian in the negative sense, for it would not provide us with an achievable conception of justice that can be attainable given reasonable limitations of human nature and of liberal democratic societies. Hence, such imaginations should be met with skepticism and caution.

Nevertheless, the commitment to reasonable pluralism is utopian in an important sense for it ensures that citizens will be safeguarded with the capacity to pursue a conception of the good of their own choosing. While it would not be possible for an entire society to unite behind a common good, a fundamental interest of citizens would still be protected, along with the ability for citizens to associate with others who share similar values, as enumerated in the first principle of justice of any realistic utopia—Rawls's principle that protects the basic liberties.[45]

---

[44] LP, 12.

[45] LP, 14. In addition to protecting the basic liberties found in a constitutional regime, Rawls argues that a realistic utopia will also ensure that the means to exercise these liberties will be provided for all (typically found in Rawls's second principle of justice—the difference principle and fair equality of opportunity).

Ultimately, when we combine these various elements contained within a realistic utopia—namely, a recognition of the practical limitations of human nature and of social life, combined with political ideals that are accessible to all and capable of providing a critical standpoint from which to judge our principles—Rawls believes we will have grounds for the reasonable *hope* in the possibility of achieving a reasonable and just society that is stable across time. Moreover, Rawls says, in his discussion of Hegel, that we will be able to *reconcile* ourselves to our society and its institutions, as opposed to merely "resigning" ourselves to them.[46] In this sense, we misunderstand the notion of a realistic utopia if we view it as a form of *tragic* compromise between realism and utopianism. Instead, a realistic utopia should illustrate a vision that can be supported by all citizens and accepted as reasonable, for it does not run contrary to—and actually supports—the fundamental interests of persons to pursue a conception of the good and develop a sense of justice, and aligns with the deepest psychological tendencies of human nature and of social cooperation. This ensures that justice will be affirmed and endorsed across time.[47]

Of course, there are some natural limitations to the idea of a realistic utopia. First, it assumes that there are favorable historical circumstances surrounding the

---

[46] JF, 3.

[47] Rawls also argues, more controversially, that justice is aligned with or "congruent" with the human good in TJ, 450-514. It is notable that the congruence argument is not mentioned in his discussion of the idea of a realistic utopia in the *Law of Peoples* and *Justice as Fairness*. Scholars believe that the main reason Rawls withdrew from this argument is because it conflicts with his commitment to reasonable pluralism. For a discussion, see Freeman, Samuel. "Congruence and the Good of Justice" in *Justice and the Social Contract*. Oxford University Press, 2007: 143-172.

development of society.[48] Conditions of extreme scarcity due to devastating natural disasters or economic collapse, or historically unfavorable events such as catastrophic war will preclude a realistic utopia from being realized. In these more unfortunate circumstances, citizens may find it difficult to see society as a system of social cooperation for mutual benefit, or their concern for safety and security will be so stark as to preclude them from forming the requisite level of trust with one another for reciprocity to shape social relations. In such conditions, an aim to restore favorable conditions will be paramount so as to ensure that justice can be possible in society once again.

A second limitation is that the implementation of a realistic utopia will not solve all questions of meaning and purpose for individuals. As Rawls remarks, "a realistic utopia...may be a social world whose many members may suffer considerable misfortune and anguish, and may be distraught by spiritual emptiness."[49] The reason for this is because Rawls does not understand political society as a "community" or "association," if we mean by such terms the idea of living together under a single unified common good.[50] While it may be imaginable that such a group of persons could exist—united and deeply fulfilled in their communal endeavor with all persons—the limitations of reasonable pluralism cannot allow for its realization. Instead, Rawls leaves questions of meaning and purpose to the freedom of individuals and their associations *within*

---

[48] JF, 84. Included in these favorable circumstances are the "circumstances of justice" which are moderate scarcity and limited benevolence, coupled with an acceptance of reasonable pluralism.
[49] LP, 127.
[50] JF, 21.

political society.[51] Hence, while a realistic utopia does not guarantee complete fulfillment in life, it affords everyone the effective opportunity to pursue his or her final ends to the greatest extent allowable by a free society.

---

[51] LP, 127.

Chapter 3: Justice and Ideal Theory

> If ideal theory is worthy of study, it must be because, as I have conjectured, it is the fundamental part of the theory of justice and essential for the nonideal part as well.[52]

1. Introduction

The purpose of this chapter is to affirm the value and necessity of ideal theory in political philosophy. As discussed in the introduction, ideal theory involves a certain methodology for determining the correct principles of justice for society. This methodology typically involves idealizing assumptions that ignore certain features of the world, or imagines hypothetical features that do not currently exist. In addition to these methodological features, ideal theory is said to be important for our understanding of how we should proceed in "nonideal" conditions of society where justice is not met. The idea is that, unless have a full understanding of what justice requires in an ideal model, we cannot address the problems posed by the more complex circumstances of social life. The task of this chapter is to evaluate these two different components of ideal theory.

An inquiry of this kind is particularly apt given the growing chasm that has appeared between ideal theorists on the one hand, who assert the primacy of ideal theory for delineating the requirements of justice, and political realists on the other, who largely eschew ideal theory and warn of its irrelevance, and even its potentially dangerous effects. To illustrate this deep disagreement, consider the following tableau

[52] TJ, 343.

of the current debate: In the realist camp, Amartya Sen argues that ideal theory is "neither necessary nor sufficient for advancing justice in society;"[53] David Wiens argues that "we should abandon ideal theory in our attempts to address actual injustices;"[54] Charles Mills and Carol Pateman claim that there is an unjustified "hegemony of 'ideal theory' in political philosophy."[55]

In support of ideal theory, John Rawls states that "ideal theory is the only basis for the systematic grasp of...pressing problems [of injustice];"[56] Allen Buchanan believes that "the task of ideal theory is to set the most important and most distant moral targets for a better future," and serve as "the ultimate standards for evaluating law.";[57] John Simmons argues that "the political philosopher's first job...is to refine and argue for an ideal of justice;"[58] Adam Swift argues that "we need fundamental, context-independent, normative philosophical claims to guide political action even in nonideal circumstances."[59]

---

[53] Sen, Amartya. "What do we want from a Theory of Justice?" *The Journal of Philosophy*, Vol. 53, No. 5, May (2006): 217.
[54] Wiens, David. "Prescribing Institutions without Ideal Theory," in *The Journal of Political Philosophy:* Vol. 20, No. 1 (2012): 45–70.
[55] Pateman, Carol and Charles Mills. *Contract and Domination.* Cambridge: Polity Press, 2007: 107. Also see Mills, Charles. "Ideal Theory as Ideology," *Hypatia* (2005): 165-184. For further criticisms, see Galston, William. "Realism in Political Theory," *European Journal of Political Theory*, 9 (2010): 385; Geuss, Raymond. *Philosophy and Real Politics.* Oxford University Press, 2008; and Williams, Bernard. *In the Beginning was the Deed: Realism and Moralism in Political Argument*, Princeton University Press, 2005.
[56] TJ, 8.
[57] Buchanan, Allen. *Justice, Legitimacy, and Self-Determination*. New York: Oxford University Press, 2004: 60.
[58] Simmons, John. "Ideal and Nonideal Theory," *Philosophy & Public Affairs* 38, No. 1 (2010): 36.
[59] Swift, Adam. "The Value of Philosophy in Nonideal Circumstances," *Social Theory and Practice*, Vol. 34, No. 3 (2008): 363. Also see Dworkin, Ronald. *Sovereign Virtue*. Harvard University Press, 2000: 172 for a discussion about the "ideal ideal world," "ideal real world" and the "real real world."

The wide array of positions with respect to the role of ideal and nonideal theory in political philosophy reflects, on my view, not only a confusion about what exactly we *mean* when we say "ideal theory" and "non-ideal" theory, but also a lack of agreement about what the proper methodology for doing political philosophy is and what role a conception of justice is supposed to serve in our normative thinking. It is only after we articulate a considered view of these questions can we begin to resolve the ideal vs. nonideal debate that has since emerged in the contemporary literature.

Given this diagnosis of the problem, this chapter will serve two aims: (1) clarify the meaning of the ideal/non-ideal distinction, and (2) argue that ideal theory, properly understood, is necessary for theorizing about justice, and is intricately connected with our obligations in so called "non-ideal" circumstances. The outline of this chapter is as follows: First, I begin with a detailed account of Rawls's understanding of ideal theory, as it is typically at the forefront of various debates. In doing so, I highlight several misunderstandings of his view and offer my own attempt to correct them in the spirit of Rawls's work. Next, I consider various objections presented by realists, who attempt to undermine Rawls's assumption that ideal theory is the proper method for theorizing about justice. I argue that all of the objections to Rawls's understanding of ideal theory fail. In doing so, I argue that Rawls's understanding of ideal theory is grounded in his understanding of a realistic utopia, an idea which governs the goals and aims of political philosophy itself.

II. Rawls and the Ideal

The main impetus for the current debate between nonideal and ideal theory stems from various components of John Rawls's work in political philosophy, so it is natural to begin our discussion of the topic with his account. While some theorists regard Rawls's treatment of the topic clear and straightforward, upon examining Rawls's work carefully, we come across numerous difficulties when attempting to account for all the cases where Rawls employs the terms "ideal" and "nonideal."[60] A sampling of some of the key ideas of Rawls's texts will suffice to demonstrate this complexity. For instance, Rawls describes in the course of his work: the definition of "ideal theory" and "nonideal theory,"[61] an "ideal conception of the person,"[62] an "ideal of society as a fair system of social cooperation,"[63] the "ideal of a well-ordered society,"[64] an "ideal of the rational and reasonable,"[65] and the "ideal of public reason,"[66] among many others.[67] Those familiar with Rawls will recognize that these are some of the most important and central ideas that govern and structure Rawls's work. It is no coincidence, then, that debates surrounding the ideal/nonideal distinction cover such a vast terrain and require a deep engagement with Rawls's underlying ideas. Nevertheless, to provide some

---

[60] Simmons (2010) makes this point clearly in one of the most thorough treatments of Rawls's ideal/nonideal theory distinction. However, even Simmons's work is limited to one portion of Rawls's theory and is thereby incomplete.

[61] JF, 13.

[62] TJ, 260.

[63] CP, 307.

[64] CP, 321.

[65] PL, 102.

[66] PL, 248.

[67] See "ideal regarding principles" (TJ, 291); a "social ideal" as opposed to an "ideal of justice" (TJ, 9); the "ideal of a social union," (TJ, 450); the "ideal of democratic citizenship" (PL, 152). We can also add "nonideal" to each of terms and generate new concepts.

structure to our inquiry, we will begin our discussion with what Rawls himself formally calls "ideal theory" proper and "nonideal theory."

(a) Rawls and Ideal Theory

One purpose of ideal theory, for Rawls, is to provide us with the most appropriate methodology for establishing the correct principles of justice that would govern the perfectly just, or "well-ordered" society.[68] The central components of Rawls's ideal theory are the two following idealizing assumptions: (1) an assumption of "full or strict compliance," and (2) an assumption of "favorable circumstances." With respect to full compliance, Rawls means that "(nearly) everyone strictly complies with, and abides by, the principles of justice."[69] Regarding "favorable circumstances," Rawls refers to the "historical, economic, and social conditions" that "make a constitutional regime possible."[70] There is much to unpack in these conditions, but for now, the general idea is that, when determining which principles of justice would be best, Rawls believes that we must begin our inquiry by assuming that everyone follows those principles of justice and that the social circumstances are favorable for justice to arise.

In what sense are these assumptions ideal? The first assumption is "idealized" in the sense that full compliance does not obtain in actual political societies. No society, currently or historically, has ever ensured strict compliance with its rules among all

---

[68] TJ, 213. A well-ordered society, for Rawls, contains several elements. First, it describes a society in which everyone agrees on the same principles of justice; second, it applies those principles to govern and order its institutions; third, it assumes that these principles are publicly acknowledged; forth, it assumes that citizens are willing and able to act upon a "sense of justice" in support of these institutions; and fifth, it describes a society that is stable for the right reasons. See Freeman, 484.

[69] JF, 13.

[70] JF, 47, 101.

citizens. The second assumption is idealized in the sense that it asks us to discount abnormal conditions, such as the existence of war and famine, when determining which principles are best—even though these are real and genuine problems that societies must face.

While it may appear strange to begin an inquiry of justice with these assumptions, it is helpful to remind ourselves that these techniques are not limited to normative theorizing, and are pervasive in the empirical sciences as well. For instance, in economic theory, there are no actual markets in which perfect competition exists. Nevertheless, the assumption of perfect competition is used prominently as a formal model that simplifies our domain of inquiry to provide some traction in tackling the problem of understanding markets and prices. Similarly, in chemistry, the ideal gas law proports to describe how ideal gases behave in "normal conditions" of standard pressure and temperature. Chemists recognize that abnormal conditions can present us with complex problems. Yet, they proceed to assume that they do not hold with the belief that uncovering an ideal gas law will ultimately shed light on how to deal with nonideal conditions when they arise.

Given this comparison, the idea of idealization should not be immediately objectionable or unfamiliar to intellectual inquiry as such. What generates significant debate, however, is *what* features should be idealized. In the sciences, it is a choice that we must make—we *choose* to idealize away friction in physics, for instance, because we believe that doing so will aid us in our understanding of fundamental physical laws. So, we must ask in our investigation of Rawls's work whether or not these idealizing assumptions actually aid us in our understanding of justice, or if they are merely hindrances that obscure its true nature.

(b) What is Nonideal Theory?

Given Rawls's understanding of ideal theory, we can then contrast it with his account of nonideal theory. The subject of nonideal theory, for Rawls, involves the unique problems that arise when conditions of (1) strict compliance or (2) favorable circumstances do not hold. These are the conditions of "partial compliance" or "unfavorable circumstances." These conditions give rise to a new and distinct set of questions for us to answer. Broadly, questions within nonideal theory address "topics as the theory of punishment, the doctrine of just war, and the justification of the various ways of opposing unjust regimes," including civil disobedience.[71] Within the subject of global justice, nonideal theory consists of developing principles for how to deal with "outlaw states" or "burdened societies," which correspond respectively to societies that fail to comply with the Law of Peoples (noncompliance), or those societies which lack sufficient resources or political will to establish a well-ordered or decent society (unfavorable circumstances).[72]

As is well known, much of Rawls's work is primarily concerned with ideal theory, with relatively little work done in nonideal theory. However, the main reason for this

---

[71] TJ, 8, quoted in Swift, Adam and Zofia Stemplowska."Ideal and Nonideal Theory," and in Estlund, David, ed. *The Oxford Handbook of Political Philosophy*. Oxford University Press, 2012: 375.
[72] LP, 90.

asymmetry is not because Rawls is insensitive or uninterested in problems of nonideal theory, but rather because he thinks that "ideal theory is...the only basis for the systematic grasp of these more pressing problems [within nonideal theory]."[73] In other words, Rawls thinks that it would be difficult to attempt solutions to the problems of nonideal theory—war, punishment, weak and unstable institutions, or deeply corrupted government—without understanding the conclusions drawn from work within ideal theory where full compliance and favorable conditions are assumed from the start. The goal for our exegesis is to establish just *why* these assumptions are necessary and how ideal theory can generate accurate guidance for the pressing problems that nonideal circumstances pose.

(c) Why Full Compliance?

The assumption of full compliance typically generates significant debate with respect to Rawls's methodological assumptions of ideal theory. And, on first glance, it seems like a puzzling assumption. Why should we think that assuming full compliance is a reliable method for determining what principles of justice we should adopt to eventually guide us in nonideal circumstances? Won't this lead us astray?

One reason to think that the full compliance assumption is problematic is that it appears to simply idealize the central problem of justice (noncompliance) away from the very start, rendering the exercise irrelevant. Realists, for example, argue that the core problem that a conception of justice must address is the problem of order and stability,

---

[73] Ibid., 8. Also quoted in Valentini, 655.

of which noncompliance is an essential threat that must be solved.[74] And so, the objection goes, if we abstract away from noncompliance, then whatever principles we come up with will not really be applicable in our world. Instead, they will be for some other world that is vastly different from our own. David Schmidtz presents this point as follows: "The trouble with ideas about what is fair in worlds without compliance problems is that they are ideas about an ideal problem, and not a real one."[75] Because of this, realists caution that any attempt to apply these ideally constructed principles framed under perfect compliance to the "nonideal" circumstances of the actual world will tend to have disastrous consequences—after all, if they were constructed by assuming that compliance was irrelevant from the very start, why should we think that they will solve problems rather than exacerbate them?

Let us consider an example to help motivate the problem. Suppose I am searching for the best principles of justice. I start with the belief that I am permitted to idealize away problems of noncompliance and begin with the assumption that everyone will adhere to my principles. Moreover, I am entitled to favorable circumstances to ensure that abnormal factors do not interfere with the realization of a society governed by these principles. I then proclaim: "Since I do not have to worry about compliance, I assert that the ideal principle of justice is one in which everyone should proclaim their faith in the Christian God and be rewarded according to the Christian understanding of

---

[74] See Williams, Bernard. *In the Beginning Was the Deed: Realism and Moralism in Political Argument*. Princeton University Press, 2005. Also, Hobbes, Thomas. *Leviathan*, ed. by Richard Tuck. Cambridge University Press, 2007.

[75] Schmidtz, David. "Ideal Theory: What it is and What it Needs to be," *Ethics* vol. 121, no. 4 (2011): 778.

virtue and merit." To anyone who would object to my principle by claiming that not everyone is a Christian, I can merely say, "That is a problem for *nonideal* theory and not my concern here. I am modelling the perfectly just society, and if compliance is not an obstacle, then everyone affirming one religious doctrine is ideal." To anyone who claims that Christian teachings are not always available to people, I can invoke the "favorable conditions" clause, and assume that everyone has reasonable access to Bibles, Christian Churches, and the willingness and aptness to put their faith in God. And now, with the true principles of justice at hand constructed using ideal theory, I can move to nonideal theory and address the problem of heathens (partial compliance) or "barbaric" and "uncivilized" nations who have not heard the word of God (unfavorable conditions).

Framed this way, the idealizing assumption of full compliance looks troubling. It appears to have the power to render moot any number of barriers that may apply in the real world for complying with principles of justice. As such, the results will be catastrophic when we attempt to implement them for society. As William Galston warns, "if one supposes that a republic of virtue is within reach, then the failure to attain it reflects either inadequate effort or deliberate but remediable human perversity. Acting on this belief is bound to end in oppression, even terror."[76] The idea here is that tyranny is the inevitable conclusion to our attempts to apply an ideal theory of justice that is based on an implausible assumption of what humans are capable of achieving. And since the full compliance assumption *conceals* the obstacles and limits on human

[76] Galston, 395.

capabilities, any attempt to approach that ideal will result in policies that may severely threaten liberty as trial upon trial is met with only the recalcitrance of human imperfections.

We can describe this problem more expansively by postulating a vast array of principles of justice that would pass through the strict compliance assumption with little resistance or objection at the level of ideal theory: (a) perfect equality of resources—by assuming everyone will comply with taxing their income to the point of equality; (b) theocratic/communitarian principles—by assuming that everyone will comply with the dictates of a religion or cultural standard, or (c) perfectionism—by assuming that everyone will acknowledge the same universal standard of goodness. If these principles can ignore any problems of adherence in their formulation, the realists remind us that it is easy to see how a transition into nonideal circumstances armed with these principles could generate significant resistance.[77]

So, the realists wonder, how can the full compliance assumption in Rawlsian ideal theory be useful? It seems to be an inert exercise that cannot yield satisfactory conclusions about what we should do in the nonideal world since it idealizes away core problems of justice.[78]

---

[77] See Galston, 405 for a broad attack on the full compliance test that presents some of these worries.
[78] While some philosophers, such as G.A. Cohen, would welcome the challenge to argue for or against principles of justice solely on their rational merits, absent any constraints of compliance, surely Rawls would not regard this as one of his goals. I will address Cohen's position in a later chapter. But, briefly, Cohen would argue that idealizing away noncompliance in the sense described would allow us to evaluate the merits of each principle of justice itself, without it being tainted by considerations of empirical limitations of feasibility. Moreover, Cohen would claim that he could show that some principles in our proposed list—such as perfectionism or communitarianism—would fail on purely rational or intuitionist

To answer the realist objection, we must probe a bit more deeply into the justifying reasons Rawls provides for his assumption of full compliance. In doing so, we will see how the aforementioned objections rest on a misunderstanding of Rawls's view.

(d) The Importance of Full Compliance: The Stability Condition

For Rawls, one reason for assuming full compliance in ideal theory is to simplify our analysis of the stability condition that Rawls emphasizes for principles of justice. It is not to be used as a formal model to construct a picture of what the perfect society would look like absent all constraints related to compliance whatsoever. This is a significant source of error in criticisms of Rawls so it is worth explicating at length Rawls's view of the stability condition and how the assumption of full compliance aids us in testing it.

Rawls's stability condition represents a substantive constraint—if not the most neglected substantive constraint—on our principles of justice.[79] It is based on the idea that principles of justice must endure over time and gain reliable adherence by citizens if they are to be suitable candidates for the regulation of society. This is because we are not interested in principles of justice that could only enjoy momentary success or those that would require miraculous fortune to achieve. Nor are we interested in principles of justice that could only be adhered to with great difficulty through the disfigurement of our moral psychology. Instead, for Rawls, we aim to discover principles of justice that

---

grounds, ultimately yielding his favored principle of justice—luck egalitarianism--which requires inequalities due to luck to be neutralized. See Cohen, G.A. *Rescuing Justice and Equality*. Harvard University Press, 2008.

[79] TJ, 397-404, 434-441.

reliably connect with the deep and internal psychological mechanisms of persons. This ensures that citizens will adequately develop a sense of justice to adhere to its mandates over time. Rawls states:

> It is evident that stability is a desirable feature of moral conceptions...However attractive a conception of justice might be on other grounds, it is seriously defective if the principles of moral psychology are such that it fails to engender in humans beings the requisite desire to act upon it.[80]

Given that Rawls focuses on the compatibility of principles of justice with human motivational capacities, Rawls is actually in agreement with many realists who argue that we must be concerned with the compliance question with respect to justice as it relates to the reasons why citizens may or may not be able to comply with the requirements of justice.

In addition to connecting the stability of justice to moral psychology and human nature, Rawls, more controversially, argues that the stability of justice can only be safeguarded if justice can be shown to be part of the human good—known in Rawlsian scholarship as the congruence argument.[81] While I cannot fully explicate this argument here,[82] I will briefly remark that the main impetus for this additional component is the hope that justice can be internally endorsed as a good for us, as opposed to merely being accepted instrumentally. The worry is that, if it turns out that justice is detrimental or disconnected from our good, or if it cannot be endorsed from within,

---

[80] TJ, 398.

[81] See TJ, Part III.

[82] For a more complete version of this argument, see Freeman, Samuel. *Justice and the Social Contract.* Oxford University Press, 2007: 143-172.

then we can only be externally motivated into accepting its demands through fear and threats, or bargaining and compromise.[83] Rawls rejects this basis for stability and attempts to show how acting for the sake of justice enables us to realize the more fundamental aspects of our moral personality, whatever conception of the good we happen to choose. As such, it is central to the good of all rational and reasonable persons. Rawls couples this with the "Aristotelian Principle," according to which we derive pleasure and satisfaction from the development of our higher order capacities, including the sense of justice. Consequently, developing our capacity to act for the sake of justice can be experienced as a highest-order good by all.[84]

We have now shown that Rawls's stability condition consists of two limitations on principles of justice: (1) they must be compatible with human nature and moral psychology, and (2) they must be capable of being affirmed within our good. Taken together, the two elements of Rawls's concern with stability has both an empirical and a normative component and corresponds directly to the realistic and utopian threads of Rawls's project.

With the full idea of the stability condition in mind, we can now return to the importance of the full compliance assumption within Rawls's ideal theory. As we have already shown, it would be a mistake to claim that Rawls engages in the assumption of full compliance in order to conceal all the reasons why people fail to comply with a

---

[83] Similar to, say, Hobbes's conception of stability as based upon "compromise, coercion and a *modus vivendi* among essentially conflicting interests," see Freeman (2006), 102.
[84] See TJ, 372-380 for a discussion of the Aristotelian Principle and its relationship to the sense of justice and the good of persons.

principle of justice. Instead, Rawls utilizes ideal theory to help us evaluate methodically which principles, when strictly complied with, could *be realistically stable*, given features of human nature and our moral psychology. If it turns out that our proposed principles would fail to be supported by citizens through reliable psychological mechanisms, they will be rejected. As John Simmons puts it,

> The strict compliance assumption is designed only to allow us to imagine the results of getting 'up and running' the institutions embodying different conceptions of justice, which requires imagining that those subject to those institutions support and comply with them, at least initially. But it may turn out that some conceptions...'exceed the capacity of human nature,' such that long-term support and compliance are unlikely or impossible.[85]

In other words, the assumption of full compliance is a heuristic device to test whether our candidate principles of justice would endure through time, or if they would instead "exceed the capacity of human nature." Freeman corroborates:

> The stability problem for Rawls requires showing how a conception of justice is realistically possible given human nature and certain fixed conditions of social life. To do so, Rawls assumes the ideal case of a well-ordered society [in which strict compliance is a component]. If a conception of justice is not workable there, then it is not feasible under less than ideal conditions.[86]

So, the full compliance condition enables us to test the workability and feasibility of our various principles of justice by modelling them in a well-ordered society. If it turns out that the strains on our moral psychology are too great, or if justice cannot be secured

---

[85] Simmons (2010), 9. Simmons quotes Rawls at TJ, 176.

[86] Freeman, Samuel. "Introduction: John Rawls—An Overview," in *The Cambridge Companion to Rawls*, Cambridge University Press, 2003: 23.

through internal motivations that are connect with our good, then we should reject the principle.

(e) The Importance of Full Compliance: Removal of Confounding Variables

In addition to aiding us in assessing the stability of a principle of justice, the full compliance assumption of Rawls's ideal theory enables us to isolate the relevant normative features of a principle when comparing it to another conception of justice. As Simmons points out,

> If we compare the operation of societies ordered by competing principles of justice while assuming strict compliance with those principles, the different effects we observe can reasonably be taken to be wholly the responsibility of the different ordering principles themselves. If instead we try to evaluate principles in terms of how societies governed by them would operate with a 'normal' amount of noncompliance with them, we will likely find that our evaluations yield quite indeterminate results.[87]

What Simmons has in mind here is that, by assuming full compliance, we can be confident that our acceptance or rejection of a principle is *due to normative features of the principle itself*, and not a confounding variable. As such, the full compliance condition allows us to compare different conceptions of justice against one another on equal footing.

By way of illustration, we can examine an analogy in the methodology of the sciences to demonstrate the importance of isolating variables.[88] Suppose I wanted to test the effectiveness of two different social policies on educational outcomes in low-income neighborhoods. It is a basic methodological rule in the social sciences that,

---

[87] Simmons (2010), 8-9.
[88] I thank Kok-Chor Tan for drawing my attention to this comparison with the sciences.

when we test the competing policies, we ensure that the relevant variables are the same in both cases. So, if we test policy A on school system *S*, and test policy B on school system *T*, we would do well to ensure that the relevant variables in *S* and *T* are identical—say the level of income and test scores in each school district.[89] Otherwise, it would be extremely difficult to measure the successfulness of the two policies in any reliable and convincing manner.

Through this analogy, we can see that Rawls's assumption of full compliance is one way of holding the relevant conditions in society constant so that we can more effectively gauge the outcomes of different principles of justice. If we do not hold compliance constant, it will be difficult to disentangle all the various causes and factors that may explain noncompliance—some of which may have little to do with the normative content of the principles. Noncompliance, for instance, might be the result of a lack of trust in institutions due to past political failures, or perhaps due to the prevalence of false information in society, or maybe corrupt politicians. These problems of noncompliance are not relevant in the right way to our assessment of principles of justice. We want to test for noncompliance that is due to the principles of justice themselves, and not these other reasons. As such, we assume full compliance to isolate and better evaluate the normative content.

[89] Of course, even these two variables are not sufficient to establish the preference of one policy over another, for there may still be other hidden or unknown variables that affected the results.

(f) The Importance of Assuming Favorable Circumstances

We are now in a position to segue into Rawls's second idealizing assumption in ideal theory: the assumption of "favorable circumstances." The rationale for assuming favorable circumstances is similar to the reasoning for the assumption of full compliance: we want to ensure that we are accurately evaluating our principles of justice without undue influence of irrelevant factors. These irrelevant factors will become evident as we explicate what Rawls means by "favorable circumstances."

By "favorable circumstances," Rawls means two different things. First, Rawls includes what he calls the "circumstances of justice" which are "the normal conditions under which human cooperation is both possible and necessary."[90] Rawls focuses on the conditions of social cooperation because they are the conditions in which concerns of justice arise. This requires the capacity for persons to view their cooperative endeavors as capable of being governed by fairness and reciprocity. If we find ourselves in unfavorable circumstances—such as a brutal state of war, or a condition of resource scarcity due to catastrophic natural disaster, or any other destabilizing condition that makes social cooperation impossible—it will be difficult for persons to acquire the requisite motivation to act for the sake of justice at all.[91]

To illustrate, in a longstanding condition of civil war, people may reject distributive principles that apply to their adversaries; or, in conditions of global

---

[90] TJ, 109. The circumstances of justice include "limited beneficence" and "moderate scarcity of resources."
[91] TJ, 110.

catastrophe, people may refuse to give up resources to benefit others when they themselves have a tenuous possession of the goods necessary for their own livelihood. In these conditions, people will not generally be willing to act for the sake of upholding just institutions in society that govern the relations of social cooperation. Instead, they will fall back on other norms for action such as simple prudence or self-preservation.[92] As a result, if we do not assume favorable conditions, it will be difficult to formulate what the best principle of *justice* is, given that people will not develop the requisite disposition to see their social activity as constrained by justice in the first place.

Second, Rawls includes in "favorable circumstances," the "historical, economic, and social conditions" that "make a constitutional regime possible."[93] These conditions include the "economics means...education, or the main skills needed to run an economic regime."[94] As such, unfavorable circumstances may include conditions in which citizens may not have a sufficient historical memory or historical precedent for newly erected democratic institutions; or, societies may lack the economic resources to institute and implement a just intuitional regime; or, citizens may lack the background framework and skills necessary for citizens to reform and refine their institutions through the political process.

---

[92] See Hume's discussion of the circumstances of justice for a similar type of account in conditions of extreme scarcity. Hume, David. *Enquiry Concerning Principles of Morals*, ed. by Tom L. Beauchamp. Oxford University Press, 1998: 3.12. I will return to this idea in greater detail in later chapters. Also see a discussion of the state of war in Hobbes, Thomas. *Leviathan*. Chapter XIII: 86-90.

[93] JF, 47, 101.

[94] JF, 47. As quoted in Stemplowska, Zofia and Adam Swift. "Rawls on Ideal and Nonideal Theory," in *A Companion to Rawls*, ed. By Jon Mandle and David Reidy. Wiley, Blackwell: 2014: 115.

In general, favorable circumstances are designed to mirror the general conditions most citizens in liberal democratic societies find themselves in already. This elegantly corresponds to Rawls's realistic elements of his project, for he views his task to find principles of justice that answer to our current political situation, and not for some foreign or unfortunate condition of society. While "less happy conditions" would certainly be important problems for society to address, Rawls believes that we must work out principles of justice for the general case in ideal theory first before proceeding to handle these other cases.[95]

This realistic strand in Rawls's favorable conditions assumption also relates to another important limiting factor in Rawls's project. Rawls believes that constructing principles of justice that apply to "all possible circumstances" is a misguided approach, and will likely yield mistaken principles. This is because, for Rawls, we are not interested in the question: "What principles of justice apply universally across all contexts?" Instead, Rawls says:

> We focus on ideal theory because the current conflict in democratic thought is in good part a conflict about what conception of justice is most appropriate *for a democratic society under reasonably favorable conditions.* This is clear from what, for our purposes, we called the fundamental question of political philosophy.[96]

It would be a mistake, then, to understand principles of justice to be applicable everywhere and in all contexts—i.e. in times of famine, or in a previous historical era that does not have a template for democratic institutions. Of course, this does not

---

[95] TJ, 216.
[96] JF, 13 [emphasis added].

mean that *no* principles can guide conduct in these circumstances—it is just that these principles will be different from the principles of justice that are applicable to democratic societies in favorable conditions. In this sense, Rawls's project is more limited in scope.

To summarize, Rawls's two assumptions in ideal theory are designed to accomplish the following tasks: (1) serve as a heuristic device for evaluating the stability condition on principles of justice, and (2) aid us in isolating the relevant variables and eliminating the confounding variables when testing and comparing principles of justice. In no way are Rawls's idealizing assumptions designed to ignore problems of feasibility or problems of noncompliance. Quite the contrary, by effectively testing and comparing principles of justice in the ideal case, we can establish whether or not it will be possible that such principles will be feasible and complied with *in the actual world*. For if such principles fail the stability test even in favorable circumstances, then we have good reason to reject these proposed principles on the grounds that they will not be tolerable for us when we attempt to implement them in nonideal circumstances. In this regard, Rawls's ideal theory is grounded in a concern with the constraints of realism and serve to provide coherence to Rawls's conception of justice as a realistic utopia.

(g) An Illustration of Ideal Theory: Rawls's Rejection of Utilitarianism

Let us provide an illustration to see how Rawls's methodology of ideal theory is supposed to yield judgments on competing principles of justice. Given the importance of utilitarianism, and of Rawls's attempts to provide an alternative to it with his two principles of justice, it is a good choice for evaluating the merits of Rawls's methodology.[97] When assessing utilitarianism as a candidate for a principle of justice, we begin by assuming strict compliance with its principles in a well-ordered society with favorable conditions. Next, we then test the stability requirement by evaluating whether or not citizens can develop the requisite sense of justice and motivational capacities to adhere to and endorse such principles over time. To aid us in this test, we can ask ourselves the following questions:

(1) Is it feasible for persons to reliably comply with utilitarian principles?
(2) What are the primary reasons for why citizens are able to comply with it?
(3) It utilitarianism compatible with moral psychology and human nature?
(4) Is utilitarianism compatible with the human good or does it frustrate it? [98]

With respect to the first question, Rawls does not believe that the principle of utility is feasible for citizens to reliably accept.[99] In a society in which everyone strictly complies with utilitarian principles, Rawls believes there will be circumstances in which persons will be required to sacrifice some of their rights, liberties, or opportunities if doing so would be in the interests of the greater good. Rawls couples this premise with an appeal to what he calls the "strains of commitment," which is a recognition by individuals that there will be certain outcomes that are unacceptable to them given

---

[97] Rawls believes that one of the main goals of his *Theory of Justice* is to provide a systematic alternative to utilitarianism. See TJ, xvii. While Rawls's main apparatus is the use of the original position and the veil of ignorance to establish his main argument against utilitarianism, the components of ideal theory and stability are an important corollary to this argument and will be the focus of this section. For a more complete account of this relationship, see Scheffler, Samuel. "Rawls and Utilitarianism," in *A Companion to Rawls*, ed. by Samuel Freeman. Cambridge University Press, 2003.

[98] There are, of course, other questions that deliberators must ask when considering which principles of justice are superior. However, the questions above are distinctly related to the stability condition and the purposes of strict compliance, so I have highlighted these.

[99] TJ, 137-139. See Freeman (2006): 98-102 for a more complete version of this argument.

their commitment to their own rational plan of life, and their sense of self-respect.[100] Requiring individuals to forgo core opportunities to advance their conception of the good for the sake of those who may already have a greater share violates these strains of commitment—it would be difficult for citizens who view society as a system of fair cooperation to accept such a sacrifice as it does not adequately respect their own contribution to it, and nor does it offer enough protection to the fundamental interests in pursuing a rational plan of life. As such, Rawls believes that persons would reject utilitarianism, for "having to acquiesce in a loss of freedom over the course of their life for the sake of a greater good enjoyed by others," would be unacceptable.[101]

One common objection to Rawls's criticism of utilitarianism here is that the principle of utility will not require the sacrifices imagined by Rawls. That is, utilitarians hold that it is generally the case that our basic liberties and rights will be respected in the normal conditions of political society, and citizens will not be asked to forgo them or an adequate share of resources and opportunities for the sake of others, let alone the already better-off.[102] It would only be through imagined or drastic scenarios in which these undue sacrifices would ever be required and so are not relevant for our purposes.

---

[100] TJ, 153-160. Rawls says persons "cannot enter into agreements that may have consequences they cannot accept. They will avoid those that they can adhere to only with great difficulty....given knowledge of human psychology," TJ, 153.

[101] TJ, 154.

[102] In fact, on Peter Singer's account of utilitarianism, it is far more likely to be the reverse—that citizens who are well-off are much more likely to be asked to give significant portions of their resources to the worst-off. See Singer, Peter. "Famine, Affluence and Morality," *Philosophy and Public Affairs* vol. 1, no. 3, (1972): 229-243. However, this may only appear to be the case given significant departures from justice in our current society. In a well-ordered society governed by utilitarianism in which strict compliance was held, the sacrifices would not be as stark.

This is an important objection because we are working within ideal theory and with the assumption of favorable circumstances. As such, it would be inappropriate to reject utilitarianism if we only tested it using contrived counterexamples that would not likely emerge in the normal course of political society.[103] Instead, we must aim to show how the endorsement of utilitarianism by citizens would generate problems of stability given the general facts of human beings and their social world. A simple counterexample in an extreme scenario will not suffice.

Given this condition, how does Rawls demonstrate that utilitarianism requires the sacrifice of some rights, liberties and opportunities for the sake of others *within ideal theory*? Rawls accomplishes this task, not by presenting us with specific hypothetical counterexamples—they would not be sufficiently general for the purposes of ideal theory—but by describing the decision-making model of utilitarianism itself and the conception of the person that underlies the methodology. Upon doing so, we end up with a portrait of an ideal legislator who will not be represented as having the requisite concerns to safeguard our basic liberties, rights and opportunities and to

---

[103] It is doubtful that Rawls had much interest in hypothetical counterexamples designed to probe the limits of utilitarianism—examples such as the dangers of hospital patients being killed for their organs, or the dilemma of Jim and the Indians. While such counterexamples may be appropriate in other contexts, they are not particularly illuminating for the establishment of principles of justice to govern our institutions. By the same token, it would also be inappropriate to reject deontological accounts of rights through the same kinds of examples. For instance, Amartya Sen has sought to undercut deontological protections of rights by pointing out a potential hypocrisy in Rawls who endorses the "supreme emergency exception" to the rights of innocent persons in his *Law of Peoples*. See LP, 98-99. Sen argues: "Once such an exception is made, it is not clear what remains of the basic priorities in his theory of justice." See Sen, Amartya. *The Idea of Justice*. Harvard University Press, 2009: 85. While Sen is referring to Robert Nozick's own moral catastrophe exception, Sen also raises the same question for Rawls. Also mentioned in Freeman, Samuel. "A New Theory of Justice," *New York Review of Books*, October 14th, 2010. The reply here is that ideal theory assumes strict compliance and favorable circumstances first, and then is utilized at a later stage to address extreme cases.

respect our fundamental interests in pursuing our own rational life plan. In other words, Rawls aims to show that utilitarianism's unacceptability and unreasonableness to us is endemic to the theory itself as it is understood in its ideal conditions.

The dominant method for understanding how utilitarianism is to be applied for the purposes of justice and the organization of social institutions is through the "impartial spectator" model, whereby we imagine one perfectly rational and sympathetic person who experiences the desires of everyone and makes decisions that accurately incorporate the desires of all.[104] On this model, "many persons are fused into one," and the impartial spectator represents "the desires of all persons into one coherent system of desire."[105] What results is the "conflating of all persons into one through the imaginative acts of the impartial sympathetic spectator."[106] Rawls asserts that this model obliterates the "distinction between persons," and later argues that this model of the ideal legislator only represents "the ethic of perfect altruists."[107]

Why might Rawls assert that it is only perfect altruists that utilitarianism would be best suited for? It is because the only social organization that would endorse and accept such a model would be an association of bees or ants, which regularly requires the sacrifice of the good of the individual for the sake of the hive with little regard to the final ends of the singular ant or bee. But since bees and ants are much more prosocial in nature—perhaps not perfect altruists in the strict sense, but far closer than we are—

---

[104] This is primarily with respect to "classical utilitarianism." See Smith, Adam. *Theory of Moral Sentiments*, ed. by D.D. Raphael and A.L. Macfie. Oxford University Press, 1976.

[105] TJ, 24. Quoted and discussed by Scheffler (2003): 429-430.

[106] TJ, 24.

[107] TJ, 25, 164.

the impartial spectator model would be appropriate and applicable to them. In contrast, this "hive mind" approach to the organization of our institutions and policies would be wholly unacceptable to us, even if we acknowledged that it would maximize overall happiness. This is because, unlike ants, we *do* care about how our individual lives turn out, and we do not completely regard our good as merely a part of the whole. This, of course, does not mean that we are entirely selfish, but rather that we care enough about our own lives such that we require special protections to ensure that great sacrifices are not genuine and expected possibilities of our social life.

It is in this sense that Rawls believes that persons would reject utilitarianism, for the ideal model of the impartial spectator does not provide any assurances to persons that their rational plan of life will be safeguarded. As such, persons will have great difficulty endorsing and adhering to the principle of utility over time, and the stability of the system will be threatened.[108]

Utilitarians will likely reply to Rawls's argument here in one of two ways. First, they may reiterate that in the normal circumstances of political life, these sacrifices will not be required, and so the idealizing assumption of favorable circumstances should exclude it from consideration. Or, they may argue that, since there are few cases in

---

[108] The example illustrated here is applicable only to "classical utilitarianism" and not modern utilitarians who adopt the principle of average utility as the fundamental principle of justice. Rawls's argument in the second case is that persons would only accept the principle of average utility if we adopted a conception of the person who had "no aversion to risk," TJ, 165. This is because Rawls believes that the principle of average utility entails that citizens gamble with their conception of the good and their life prospects with the hope that they do not end up on the losing end. But, according to Rawls, this would be unacceptable to us, as we are not wanton enough to gamble with something of such fundamental importance to us. As such, the modern brand of utilitarianism would only be fitting for an agent who did not care very much for his own rational life plan—an agent quite unlike ourselves. TJ, 137-139. Also see Scheffler (2003): 434.

which citizens will be asked to sacrifice their good for the sake of others, it will not upset the overall stability of society—that is, there would be strong enough mechanisms to ensure the endorsement of utilitarian principles over time despite these sacrifices that citizens must occasionally make.

With respect to the first reply, this obscures the importance of the favorable circumstances clause. Suppose we compare utilitarianism with Rawls's first principle of justice, whereby the basic liberties and their priority are established right from the start as a primary safeguard. Many utilitarians object to these prioritarian systems for being insensitive to empirical circumstances where we would surely do better to sacrifice one person's rights in order to avoid great catastrophe to political society.[109] Yet, by parity of reasoning, what prevents Rawls from invoking the favorable conditions clause in this circumstance in order to deflect this criticism in the same way? To avoid this stalemate, we should strive to evaluate the core mechanisms within each normative framework and see which conception best coheres with our conception of ourselves and of our moral psychology. We have already demonstrated how utilitarianism is most fit for perfect altruists given its model of the ideal spectator, and that there is a disconnect between it and our own conception of ourselves. This dissonance generates some difficulty in our expectation that citizens would reliably develop the relevant motives to endorse and support it over time. After all, human beings *are not bees or ants*, so why should we be confident in a conception of justice that does not "take men are they

---

[109] As mentioned in fn. 53, see Sen (2009): 85.

are?"[110] and instead requires us to be governed by institutions that are designed to aggregate our ends without regard to which ends are sacrificed and which are preserved?

We can now address the second possible reply by utilitarians—the argument that it is possible for stability to be maintained in a society governed by utilitarian principles, even if it requires persons to sometimes sacrifice their own rights and liberties for the sake of others. The basis for this objection is rooted in the observation that people regularly *comply* with principles that require great sacrifices for the sake of others in a variety of contexts.[111] For example, the worst-off members across most societies throughout history have been asked to sacrifice for the sake of those with more power and wealth in society. So, the objection goes, is stability truly undermined by utilitarian principles?[112]

Rawls's reply here involves the idea of "stability for the right reasons."[113] As we have explored, a major undercurrent in Rawls's thought is to show how stability based on internal endorsement and a compatibility with the human good and moral psychology will be stronger than stability based on external force, threats or other

---

[110] This is a reference to Rousseau's suggestion to "take men as they are." See Rousseau, Jean-Jacques. *The Social Contract and other Later Political Writings*, ed. and trans. by Victor Gourevitch. Cambridge University Press, 1997: 41.

[111] See Freeman (2006): 98 for this possible objection made by utilitarians.

[112] Other possibilities include hiding the true utilitarian principles from public view. As Freeman notes, Sidgwick and Parfit both employ a form of "indirect" utilitarianism whereby only the elite few understand the true principles, but the rest of society is governed by rules that protect liberty. However, this would violate the publicity condition on our principles of justice, which requires our principles to be publicly justifiable and full view for citizens. See Freeman (2010): 47-48.

[113] *PL*, xxxix.

instrumental reasons. The question for utilitarianism is, then, would the motives for its acceptance be internal or external?[114]

There are a variety of strategies for attempting to establish an internal mechanism for its endorsement. First, we might hypothesize that there are sufficient levels of altruism in society such that people could learn to accept to sacrifice their own good for the greater good of all. However, the level of altruism we find in humans is not strong enough to be relied upon to serve as the foundation of our compliance with principles of justice. Altruism is typically limited to specific partial groups, such as friends and family members, and is only sometimes realized for the sake of strangers—only some will be selfless as a saint, but others will be severely guarded in their affections. As such, altruism is not sufficiently generalized across all persons in society to ensure adequate compliance with utilitarian institutions.

Second, some utilitarians might argue that the primary internal motive for complying with a utilitarian principle would not be something like altruism, but something more akin to duty. On this account, a utilitarian could argue that it is the understanding of the moral correctness from an impartial point of view of the utilitarian principle that should itself serve as the primary motivator. Once citizens come to occupy the purely impartial point of view, they will recognize the normative force of the principle and will acknowledge and accept its bindingness upon them, despite their other motives to act in opposition to its mandates. To the extent that citizens fail to

---

[114] For further discussion of this distinction, see "Weithman, Paul. *Why Political Liberalism*, Oxford University Press, 2012: 43-51.

appreciate the correctness of these principles, we should do the best we can through education and tutelage to both strengthen the altruistic sentiments and expand their capacity for impartiality to better equip citizens to accept and affirm utilitarian principles.

In response, I believe that Rawls would argue that, while the motive to "do the right thing"—which Rawls includes within his "sense of justice"—is certainly part of our deepest human tendencies and important for stability, we cannot simply attach this motive to a conception of justice without also outlining the process by which persons come to acquire the motive itself.[115] The task for the utilitarian is to show how the moral motive to act in accordance with the principle of utility could reliably be acquired in citizens without undue difficulty. We have already discussed how there are significant obstacles related to the conception of the person that utilitarians endorse as a model for their theory. The tension between the requirements for altruism and the mixed motives that citizens act upon will create some conflicts in the realization of the utilitarian motive. Hence, it is not clear how successful our efforts at inculcation and education will have on our capacity to expand our sympathies to include all citizens within society.

In addition, it will be difficult to reconcile how the utilitarian system could be compatible with the human good—another important feature of stability for Rawls. If citizens will be asked to set aside their fundamental interests for the sake of others, we

---

[115] See TJ, Part III, esp. 429-434.

must ask how society will ensure that persons endorse this requirement. It seems likely that a utilitarian society will solve the stability problem by relying upon bargaining, compromise, or powerlessness by the minority to press their claims. For Rawls, these are not reasonable forms of motivations to ensure compliance as they entail the willingness of citizens to give up what is most important to them, whatever their rational plan of life turns out to be, for the sake of justice.[116] While such a society might be achievable for a brief period, it would not be stable for the right reasons.

Rawls's principles of justice, by comparison, do not require sacrifices of us that are deeply at odds with our own account of moral psychology and our most fundamental aims. By safeguarding our rights and liberties, and securing the opportunities and all-purpose means to exercising them through fair equality of opportunity and the difference principle, Rawls presents us with a conception of justice that secures our capacity to pursue our rational plan of life. This is not to suggest that Rawls's principles will never require sacrifices from us for the sake of others. What is important is that *these sacrifices are not based on altruism, acquiescence, or fear in the ideal well-ordered society*. Instead, they are based upon reciprocity, which is included in a fuller account of Rawls's sense of justice.

[116] We can illustrate this in the following way: if conditions changed and the powers were shifted, such burdened members would willingly alter their institutions and restructure them to better safeguard their interests. Hence, the fact that such citizens have an orientation to disrupt or destroy such institutions should indicate that the stability currently enjoyed by such a society would not be strong, even if it manages to persist. The idea would be that the stability of such a society would be "accidental" or "lucky," which are not suitable bases for endurance over time.

As we have seen, one part of the sense of justice is related to the moral sensibilities to act upon one's considered convictions about what is right to do.[117] However, there is also a more specialized sense in which Rawls employs the term.[118] Rawls also includes within it the notion of reciprocity, which involves the desire to act in accordance with the rules of fair social cooperation. Rawls states: "The sense of justice leads us to promote just schemes and to do our share in them when we believe that others, or sufficiently many of them will do theirs."[119] Rawls believes that his two principles of justice adequately express reciprocity between all citizens—requiring sacrifices of them without compromising their fundamental aims. As such, citizens will be sufficiently motivated to act upon justice in the well-ordered society.

Much more can be said about Rawls and his relationship with utilitarianism, and whether Rawls's arguments succeed.[120] However, this would divert us from the main issue at hand. The purpose of this illustration is to establish with greater clarity the purpose of the full compliance requirement in Rawls's ideal theory with respect to the stability requirement. And what it has shown is that it enables us to see with greater clarity the strength or weakness of a given principle of justice by examining whether a principle can reliably generate the basis for its own support. By assuming full

---

[117] TJ, 46, 489.
[118] For a discussion of this distinction see Sabl, Andrew. "Looking Forward to Justice: Rawlsian Civil Disobedience and its Non-Rawlsian Lessons," *Journal of Political Philosophy* vol. 9, no. 3 (2001). Also see Weithman (2012): 46.
[119] TJ, 236.
[120] See Scheffler (2003).

compliance, we are better able to test the compatibility of our principles with the limits of human nature and of the considered judgments of persons.

In this sense, Rawls's methodology comports with his commitment to a realistic utopia, for he uses ideal theory to generate the most reasonable and feasible principles of justice that are compatible with the judgments of citizens and their deepest psychological capacities and tendencies.

(h) Ideal Theory as Necessary for Nonideal Theory

We have thus far explored the first purpose of ideal theory for Rawls, which is to provide us with an adequate measure to test normative principles against one another. We are now in a position to examine the second purpose, which is to enable us to set a clear target or goal for society should unfavorable circumstances or injustice arise. Without this ideal target, we are left without a reliable guide as to what we should strive for as we make improvements in our nonideal circumstances. As Rawls states: "Until the ideal is identified...nonideal theory lacks an objective, an aim, by reference to which its queries can be answered."[121] In this sense, ideal theory provides us with a conception of justice that determines what our goals and priorities should be. For this reason, Rawls states that "ideal theory is the only basis for the systematic grasp of...pressing problems [of nonideal theory]."[122]

It is here that we see the relationship between ideal and nonideal theory more clearly spelled out. Not only does ideal theory provide a framework that informs us

---

[121] JF, 8.
[122] TJ, 8.

what we should aim at generally, but it will "also help to identify which wrongs are more grievous and hence more urgent to correct."[123] In this sense, ideal theory can generate a series of recommendations for which problems we should attempt to solve first. For instance, for utilitarians, dealing with nonideal circumstances would be relatively straightforward: those circumstances which produce the greatest amount of unhappiness should be addressed first. On the other hand, Rawlsians will assert that injustices that deprive citizens of equal liberties should be addressed first, before moving to equality of opportunity or the difference principle. Rawls states:

> The lexical ranking of the principles specifies which elements of the ideal are relatively more urgent, and the priority rules this ordering suggests are to be applied to nonideal cases as well. Thus as far as circumstances permit, we have a natural duty to remove any injustices, beginning with the most grievous as identified by the extent of the deviation from perfect justice. Of course, this idea is extremely rough. The measure of departures from the ideal is left importantly to intuition.[124]

To provide an illustration, Rawls applies this framework to his discussion of civil disobedience.[125] This example is a good choice to explore, since Rawls says that "the discussion of civil disobedience...depends upon it [ideal theory]....a deeper understanding can be gained in no other way."[126]

There are two ways in which ideal theory can aid us in addressing the problem of civil disobedience. First, it can determine whether or not civil disobedience is *justified*. Since civil disobedience is a "political act," it must be "guided and justified by political

---

[123] JF, 13.
[124] TJ, 216.
[125] TJ, 319-343.
[126] TJ, 8. Also quoted in Celikates, Robin. "Civil Disobedience as a Practice of Civic Freedom," in *On Global Citizenship*, by James Tully. Bloomsbury, 2014: 212.

principles....not principles of morality or to religious doctrines."[127] In addition, when engaging in civil disobedience, "one intends to address the sense of justice of the majority" and to declare that "the conditions of free cooperation are being violated."[128] For Rawls, the political principles we should draw upon are precisely those that determine the conditions of free cooperation—his two principles of justice. Hence, Rawls states: "there is a presumption in favor of restricting civil disobedience to serious infringements of the first principle of justice, the principle of equal liberty, and to blatant violations of the second principle, the principle of fair equality of opportunity."[129] So, for Rawls, in order to be justified in engaging in civil disobedience, one ought to press one's claims by appeal to the sense of justice of the political community through one of the principles of justice.

To contrast, without the framework of ideal theory, it would be difficult to determine the purpose and shape of a protestor's claims—is it someone who is acting selfishly by refusing to pay her taxes, or is it someone who is in good faith objecting to her disenfranchisement? On Rawls's view, the capacity for citizens to state their case through political principles that are part of our shared conception of justice aids us in categorizing acts of disobedience and what the proper response to it ought to be—should we punish a citizen with the maximum sentence, or exhibit leniency, and

[127] TJ, 321.
[128] TJ, 335.
[129] TJ, 326. Rawls argues that it is difficult to determine whether or not the difference principle is satisfied in society, and so focuses more on the egregious violations of our basic rights and liberties. See TJ, 327.

"suspend legal sanction?"[130] We require an ideal shared conception of justice to address these questions.

Second, ideal theory enables us to determine whether or not civil disobedience is *possible*. For Rawls, civil disobedience can only occur in a society that is "nearly just," which "implies that there exists a constitutional regime and a publicly recognized conception of justice."[131] However, this conception of justice need not be precisely Rawls's justice as fairness, but instead an "overlapping rather than strict consensus" between different political conceptions, so long as "these conceptions lead to similar political judgments."[132] So, while Rawls does employ the lexical priority to establish which violations are more urgent to address, he does allow that multiple conceptions of justice may be appealed to, so long as they invoke the sense of justice and to a political conception that admits special protections for liberty. However, if any of these conditions do not hold—the lack of an overlapping consensus, the inability to appeal to a sense of justice of the majority, or a seriously unjust society—then the conditions for civil disobedience will no longer obtain.[133] In such cases, "the wisdom of civil disobedience is highly problematic. For unless one can appeal to the sense of justice of the larger society, the majority may simply be aroused to more repressive measures."[134] In this sense, Rawls believes that ideal theory allows us to determine whether or not a

---

[130] TJ, 339. Rawls cites Dworkin, Ronald. "On Not Prosecuting Civil Disobedience," *The New York Review of Books*, June 6, 1968.
[131] TJ, 339.
[132] TJ, 340.
[133] TJ, 340.
[134] TJ, 339.

given act of disobedience will likely backfire, or if it will potentially serve its intended ends.

Some theorists have been critical of Rawls's attempt to move from ideal theory to address nonideal circumstances with respect to civil disobedience. For instance, Robin Celikates argues that, instead of aiding our discussions of civil disobedience, "the opposite is the case: ideal theory, far from being the only available route to a deeper understanding, undermines the very attempt."[135] According to Celikates, it is unlikely that the conditions for civil disobedience will ever satisfactorily be met given Rawls's more constrained definition, and that many actual cases of civil disobedience in society do not align with the framework outlined by Rawls. For instance, the paradigmatic acts of disobedience of Dr. Martin Luther King Jr., Mahatma Ghandi, and Henry David Thoreau do not, on Celikates's view, neatly fit into Rawls's system, for it requires us to see these acts as occurring within "nearly just" societies in which a shared conception of justice of the majority can legitimately be appealed to. But this seems at odds with the public understanding of these acts—that society was *manifestly* unjust, and that there was no recourse to a shared conception of justice of the majority.[136] Hence, Rawls's account leads us to a puzzling dilemma: either the acts of King and others were not

---

[135] Celikates (2014): 212.

[136] Celikates states: "It seems something of a stretch to claim that what are usually considered to be paradigm cases of civil disobedience – Thoreau, Gandhi and King – took place in societies that should be regarded as 'reasonably' or 'nearly just,'" p. 222. David Lyons makes a similar point when he notes that King, Ghandi and Thoreau did not themselves take their societies to be nearly just at all, and that *because* of this fact, civil disobedience was especially justified. See Lyons, David. "Moral Judgement, Historical Reality, and Civil Disobedience," *Philosophy and Public Affairs* vol. 27, no. 1 (1998): 31–49.

wise as they would likely backfire and cause greater resistance, or that other forms of resistance—more violent or disruptive—would be justified.[137]

As a result, Celikates rejects our reliance on ideal theory to aid us in handling cases of civil disobedience and that we are much better off with a ground-up approach that is "resolutely non-ideal – 'practical, critical and historical.'"[138] On this approach, civil disobedience is not best understood nor justified from our ideal conception of justice—in fact it is of little relevance to cases of civil disobedience. This is because the most challenging cases of civil disobedience arise when there is little agreement on what this ideal shared conception of justice is in the first place. As a result, we do better to work from within the current realities of society in which dissidents press contentious claims that may not neatly fit into the categories of Rawls's principles of justice. For instance, how would Rawls respond to the acts of civil disobedience for the sake of animal rights? On this point, Peter Singer argues that, on Rawls's view, since animals are not owed justice, there can be no legitimate civil disobedience.[139]

For critics of Rawls, it is not the role of the theorist to attempt to justify or condone acts of civil disobedience by first descending from a limited ideal standpoint; we run the risk of being myopic in our proclamations on nonideal circumstances. Instead, it is best to work from the bottom and begin with current instances of civil

---

[137] Celikates (2014): 222.
[138] Ibid., 225. Celikates quotes James Tully in Tully, James. *Public Philosophy in a New Key*, Two Volumes, Cambridge: Cambridge University Press, 2008: 16.
[139] Peter Singer states: "It is, he [Rawls] says, wrong to be cruel to animals, although we do not owe them justice. If we combine this view with the idea that the justification of civil disobedience must be in terms of justice, we can see that Rawls is committed to holding that no amount of cruelty to animals can justify disobedience." Singer, Peter, *Democracy and Disobedience*, Oxford: Clarendon Press, 1973: 90.

disobedience and how they are understood by a political community—usually different factions of the community will understand them differently—and seek to find the best way to reconcile them with the pluralist and disparate aims of society.

There are a variety of responses we can make to these criticisms of Rawls's application of ideal theory to nonideal circumstances. First of all, more generally, Rawls recognizes that there are limitations to our inquiry within nonideal theory, and that we must be particularly careful when executing our recommendations. Rawls says the following:

> We should not expect too much of a theory of civil disobedience, even one framed for special circumstances. Precise principles that straightaway decide actual cases are clearly out of the question. Instead a useful theory defines a perspective within which the problem of civil disobedience can be approached; it identifies the relevant considerations and helps us to assign them their correct weights in the more important instances. If a theory about these matters appear to us, on reflection, to have cleared our vision and to have made our considered judgements more coherent, then it has been worthwhile.[140]

Additionally, while it would have been a great asset to us if Rawls had continued to develop his ideas to address the wide variety of special cases that may arise within nonideal theory, we should not hold his entire framework hostage for his failure to address all problems. In this regard, I will only attempt to defend Rawls given his own defined limits of his approach.

For Rawls, the purpose of ideal theory with respect to the problem of civil disobedience is to frame and isolate the relative normative issues that are at stake when

---

[140] TJ, 320.

a problem of injustice confronts the political community and is responded to by violations of the law. It does not seek to prejudge any given act of civil disobedience by descending from above and determining its legitimacy straight away. Instead, the framework directs us to attempt a good faith effort to understand a dissenter's claims within the broader sense of justice within a community and to be attentive to whether those claims can be recast, first, as a response to violations of basic liberties.

Celikates takes issue with this approach because it requires there to be a defined sense of justice already within a community—an unlikely state of affairs—and that the community is already "nearly just." With respect to the latter point, Rawls's language may perhaps be infelicitous on this matter.[141] Rawls does not mean by "nearly just" a society without significant violations of basic liberties or without suppressed minorities. If he did mean this, it would be very curious as to why he would think civil disobedience would ever pose a special problem in these "nearly just" societies—a problem he saw important enough to devote a portion of *A Theory of Justice* toward addressing. As such, we should understand Rawls's claim here differently.

Rawls means by "nearly just" that there is an institutional framework in society that can adjudicate constitutional disputes, and that persons within society are motivated by a sense of reciprocity among its members. This need not include *all* members of society, however. So long as there is a sufficient majority of persons who *do* regard each other in this way can appeals by the minority begin to take hold.

---

[141] See Sabl (2001): 311: "Rawls's use of the phrase 'nearly just' may therefore be considered unfortunate."

Andrew Sabl calls such societies "piecewise just" societies, in which there is a dominant "in group" toward which the sense of reciprocity is the dominant attitude toward each member, and an "out group" which is excluded and subjugated.[142] A society thus characterized would be "nearly just" on Rawls's account, for there still would be a substantive sense of justice among its members that could be appealed to by subjugated minorities.

It is based upon this understanding of "nearly just" that we should evaluate Rawls's theory of civil disobedience. And in this context, Rawls's theory is very strong, for many of the common illustrations of civil disobedience—Dr. King in particular—fall within its bounds and can be justified as an oppressed minority appealing to the sense of justice of the broader political community.[143]

We can now respond to Celikates's second objection that there is rarely enough agreement on a conception of justice for Rawls's theory to be applicable to current conditions. But this is to overstate the degree of convergence that is necessary for appeals to gain traction. Rawls already admits that an overlapping consensus among different political conceptions is sufficient to comprehend and legitimize the claims of an oppressed minority within an otherwise fragmented society.[144] So long as we have an institutional framework that guarantees and enforces the importance of the basic

---

[142] Ibid., 311-12. Sabl cites Robert Dahl for making a similar point about the condition of 1950s America with respect to African Americans. Dahl, Robert. *Polyarchy*, Yale University Press, 1971: 28-29, 93-94.
[143] Rawls himself believes that Dr. King represents a good case to illustrate his own theory. While Dr. King utilized moral and religious arguments to state his case, they were nevertheless politically justifiable in the context of public reason. See PL, 250.
[144] TJ, 340.

liberties and the all-purpose means to realize them, we have largely satisfied Rawls's requirements.[145] These broad prerequisites are not meant to swiftly delegitimize or condemn acts of civil disobedience in the nonideal world, and nor are they meant to obscure and reify them. Instead, they serve as important and genuine constraints on what we can hope to achieve through the practice. If, for instance, there were a wholly divided society in which appeals to a common sense of justice would be truly impossible, this should serve as an indicator that a theory of civil disobedience is not going to be the appropriate framework to employ in these circumstances.[146] Instead, we may consider turning to a theory of violent resistance, revolution, or even succession.

Now, Rawls does not address the justification or legitimacy of these other forms of social disruptions. However, this should not be interpreted as a failure of Rawls's ideal theorizing. Instead, ideal theory can be used to demonstrate how these conditions are going to require new tools for thinking about them, as they lie outside the conditions that frame the standard conditions of justice. Indeed, one of the main benefits of ideal theory is that it represents our best attempt to isolate those features that are central to our understanding of ourselves, our society, and how they impact the requirements of justice—features such as the sense of justice, the conception of the person, an account of our fundamental aims, our basic moral motivations, and so forth.

---

[145] While Rawls does recognize that it will be more difficult to address elements of economic injustice, it is not impossible to construct a framework for addressing it. We might say that, if the economic conditions of the oppressed function to limit the reasonable exercise of the basic liberties, then the case will be more easily publicly justifiable.

[146] Rawls argues that "fragmented" societies characterized by significant "group egoisms" or "intolerant" groups that are set to destroy liberal institutions will undermine the conditions for civil disobedience, TJ, 340.

If any of these pieces are completely absent or are radically altered in society, ideal theory will direct us to seek out new frameworks until these conditions reemerge. Applied to the problem of truly drastic nonideal circumstances, the only recommendation that ideal theory may provide to us is to re-establish the conditions that are necessary for justice to regulate our society once again.[147]

These considerations should serve to largely assuage the worries that Rawls's ideal theory is too limited, shortsighted, or ineffectual in addressing problems of civil disobedience as part of nonideal theory. Even in the somewhat limited context in which Rawls outlines his theory of civil disobedience, we do not find ideal theory inert.

(i) Recap of Two Purposes of Ideal Theory

Let us pause for a moment to provide a brief recap of Rawls's conception of ideal theory before turning to more comprehensive objections to his view. Rawls can best be understood as utilizing ideal theory for both *methodological* and *goal-setting or orienting* purposes. It is methodological in the sense that he uses two "idealizing" assumptions—favorable circumstances and full compliance—in order to accurately *test* and *evaluate* principles of justice for stability in the normal course of social life. These methodological assumptions are not intended to condone the irrelevance of feasibility

---

[147] For instance, Rawls argues that ideal theory can even apply in such "unfavorable" circumstances in which the establishment of just institutions is severely limited. In such conditions, the lexical priority of the principles may "no longer hold," and that we may even be justified in holding prisoners of war as slaves if, for instance, countries were previously executing them, TJ, 215-16. Of course, this would not justify slavery *per se*; it would be viewed as a temporary *permissible transition* with the *eventual aim* of abolishing the practice itself (assuming, say, the institutions were so weak as to only be capable of this gradual form of change). Hence, Rawls says: "there may be transition cases where enslavement is better than current practice," TJ, 218.

or achievability conditions on the principles of justice. Quite the contrary, they enable us to *better test precisely those limitations* by eliminating confounding variables and isolating normative content.

On the other hand, Rawls's ideal theory is goal-setting in the sense that, once the principles of justice are chosen using this idealized methodology, we now have an "ideal" that sets the target for a society. We can then compare our current society with the ideal to gauge whether or not it is fully just. If it is not, then we are provided with a broad framework for determining how to get there by establishing which corrections are more urgent or pressing. Of course, ideal theory cannot *by itself* establish what we should do. We will need to consult the empirical sciences to eventually determine the best course of action. However, by using the ideal as a benchmark, we are better able to see the relationship between ideal and nonideal circumstances—the ideal will serve as the "end target" for these transitional periods in the nonideal circumstances of society as it eventually aims towards justice.

When we put these two purposes together—the methodological and the goal-setting—we can see how Rawls's conception of ideal theory incorporates both elements of his idea of a "realistic utopia." It is realistic in the sense that he takes seriously the goal of stability for principles of justice, which, in turn, influences his choice of idealizing assumptions. He wants to ensure that we accurately test these realistic constraints appropriately and ensure that persons can develop the requisite motives to act upon the selected principles of justice. It is utopian in the sense that it provides a goal or target that society should aim to achieve. Moreover, this goal extends beyond the status quo and "probes the limits of the realistically practicable."[148] The goal of achieving the well-ordered society is assuredly difficult, but not out of reach for us, in the sense that there is nothing in human nature or in the normal conditions of social life that can prevent us from ultimately achieving the ideally just society that is stable across time and affirms our good.

III. Objections to Rawls's Ideal Theory

Now that we have a general picture of Rawls's understanding of ideal and nonideal theory, I wish to address several broader objections that have been made against his view. First, I will respond to objections by political realists who reject Rawls's methodological assumption of full compliance. While we have discussed some of these objections in our exposition of Rawls's view, the ones presented here will be more fully developed. Second, in the next chapter, I will address objections by Amartya Sen who rejects the usefulness of the relationship between ideal and nonideal theory that Rawls articulates.

(a) Realist Objection: The Impossibility of Full Compliance

Many realists are familiar with Rawls's non-utopian elements of his theory, and agree with Rawls that principles of justice need to be constrained by features about human nature and concerns for stability. Nonetheless, realists persist in their objection

---

[148] JF, 13.

to Rawls by highlighting several ways in which he does not take the realistic constraints and goals of stability seriously enough.

First, with respect to Rawls's methodology, realists strongly reject the assumption of full compliance. Their claim is that full compliance with the requirements of justice will never obtain, even in the best of circumstances. William Galston, for instance, asserts that "realists deny that this assumption [of full compliance] is anything close to feasible, and they contend that this fact affects the way we should think about justice".[149] Noncompliance, in essence, is a permanent feature of society that cannot be overcome, even if we hold "favorable conditions" constant and take seriously the tendencies of human nature. For this reason, realists argue that noncompliance should not be idealized away.

Why do realists believe that full compliance is impossible? It cannot simply be the result of an acknowledgement that human beings are imperfect and are liable to falter in their commitments. Rawls can certainly accommodate this fact in his methodology. If Rawls's assumption of full compliance required the idealization of *all imperfections*, it would most likely be too idealistic—there are simply too many minor deviations from justice that occur over the course of normal social and political life. Rawls himself states as follows:

> Strict compliance means that (*nearly*) everyone strictly complies with, and abides by, the principles of justice. We ask in effect what a perfectly just, or *nearly just*, constitutional regime might be like, and whether it may come about and be made stable under the circumstances of justice,

[149] Galston (2010): 395.

and so under realistic, through reasonably favorable, conditions.[150]

On my interpretation of "nearly," Rawls allows for some departures from justice within the well-ordered society in which the assumption of full compliance holds. The reason this does not cause problems for Rawls is that these minor disruptions *will not destabilize the basic structure and institutions of society*. Society has internal mechanisms for returning to an equilibrium state when faced with offsetting conditions. Indeed, if the structure of society could be so easily dislodged by a few departures from justice, it would be miraculous that society itself could even be formed. As such, the assumption of full compliance need not idealize away these imperfections—they are inconsequential in our ability to evaluate the stability of society when we test our principles of justice. Given this caveat in Rawls, we should understand the realist objection differently.

Instead, realists object to the full compliance condition due to a much more substantive reason that is related to the necessity of conflict that characterizes democratic life. As Jeremy Waldron argues, Rawls is not sensitive enough to the fact of *deep disagreement*—not just about what the good life consists in, but also about *the nature and demands of justice itself*.[151] In other words, the problem with the full compliance condition is that, even in the best of circumstances, citizens will not agree on the basic principles of justice to govern society. Moreover, it will not simply be an

---

[150] JF, 13, emphasis added.

[151] See Waldron, Jeremy. *Law and Disagreement*. Oxford: Clarendon, 1999: 102. Also see Mason, Andrew. "Rawlsian Theory and the Circumstances of Politics," *Political Theory* 38, no. 5 (2010): 658-683.

inconsequential minority. The scope of disagreement will be significant such that the institutions of society will ebb and flow between various mixed conceptions of justice depending upon various circumstances in society.

What are some of these reasons for this deeper skepticism about convergence on principles of justice? Steve Elkin, building upon Jeremy Waldron's idea of the "circumstances of politics," argues the following:

> [The circumstances of politics consists in] states of affairs in which there is a large aggregation of people who (1) have conflicting purposes that engender more or less serious conflict; (2) are given to attempts to use political power to further their own purposes and those of people with whom they identify; (3) are inclined to use political power to subordinate others; and (4) are sometimes given to words and actions that suggest that they value limiting the use of political power by law and harnessing it to public purposes.[152]

In other words, realists tend to highlight the partial and self-serving aspects of human nature, and how the political process magnifies and exacerbates these tendencies that inhibit the possibility for agreement. Consequently, they reject Rawls's project to seek principles of justice that can garner unanimous support, and instead propose alternative solutions given the problem of deep disagreement.

What are some of these alternatives? Bernard Williams and William Galston, for instance, have indicated that for liberal societies perhaps the best we can hope for is a *modus vivendi*, which is a contingent agreement based on the mutual interests of

---

[152]Elkin, Stephen. *Reconstructing the Commercial Republic: Constitutional Design after Madison*, University of Chicago Press, 2006: 254-55. Cited in Galston (2010): 391.

conflicting parties, typically in the form of a compromise or political bargain.[153] Rawls certainly rejects these kinds of agreements, as they represent inherently unstable arrangements—if circumstances were to change, and interests shift, parties would break the agreement and instability would ensue.[154] Nevertheless, Galston claims: "When conjoined to pessimism about the possibility of purely rational consensus, the need to abate conflict implies a more favorable stance toward coordination through modus vivendi."[155] And Williams echoes: "The very phrase 'a mere *modus vivendi*' suggests a certain distance from the political; experience suggests that those who enjoy such a thing are already lucky."[156]

Realists' pessimism about agreement also spills over into the second purpose of ideal theory for Rawls—that of setting a goal for reform in nonideal circumstances. After all, if consensus is not possible, even in the best of circumstances, then it is unclear how fruitful the methodology is in generating a roadmap for how to proceed in nonideal circumstances. At best, Rawls's ideal theory might allow us to better appreciate how each conception of justice faces its own unique set of challenges for adherence; but at worst, it will yield false or illusory targets that cannot ever be attained, no matter what the circumstances. As a result, Rawls's ideal theory could potentially be dangerous,

---

[153] See also McCabe, David. *Modus Vivendi Liberalism: Theory and Practice*, Cambridge University Press, 2014.
[154] PL, 147.
[155] Galston (2010): 397.
[156] Williams, Bernard. *In the Beginning Was the Deed: Realism and Moralism in Political Argument*. Princeton University Press, 2005: 2, fn. 2.

perpetually tempting us with a vision that is forever out of reach and providing us with mistaken tasks for reform.

Given these charges against Rawls, Steve Elkin concludes the following:

> We do not best grasp the nub of partial compliance theory [nonideal theory] by focusing on ideal theory. Rather, we can best understand partial compliance when we understand just why there can only be partial compliance, and what we need to do to achieve even this modest state of affairs.[157]

Hence, for realists, the problems unique to nonideal theory can only be worked out from within nonideal theory itself, by examining why noncompliance is endemic to human life and figuring out how we can best structure institutions so that stability and order can be maintained in civil society in the face of persistent disagreement.

To briefly summarize, implicit in the realist objection is the view that incorrigible disagreement must disqualify Rawls's ideal theory of justice—both in methodology and in goal-setting. The methodology is faulty for it idealizes away a feature of society, namely noncompliance, which is central to the problem of justice. It would be akin to idealizing away features of human nature or the circumstances of justice. As a result, when we test Rawls's favored principles of justice for stability when we assume strict compliance, stability would not, in fact, be possible. In turn, realists then reject Rawls's aspirational role or goal-setting aim of his ideal theory; they assert that it will only cause harm and chaos to insist upon an ideal that is unachievable for us. As a result, they

[157] Elkin (2006): 255, cited by Galston (2010): 395.

advocate more realistic achievements such as a modus vivendi as a suitable goal for political life.

(b) Reply to Realists: The Transition from *A Theory of Justice* to *Political Liberalism*

What should we make of this critique? Should the persistence of deep disagreement affect our method for theorizing about principles of justice? Does it tarnish Rawls's goal to provide us with an ideal to guide our action in nonideal circumstances? The basis for my reply here will be one that relates to Rawls's transition from *A Theory of Justice* to *Political Liberalism* and the strategies Rawls employs to cope with the problem of disagreement in society.[158]

In *Political Liberalism,* Rawls sought to address a substantial problem faced in liberal democratic societies. Rawls states the problem as such:

> How is it possible that there may exist over time a stable and just society of free and equal citizens profoundly divided by reasonable though incompatible religious, philosophical, and moral doctrines?[159]

In asking this question, Rawls affirms what he calls "the fact of reasonable pluralism," which is an inevitable feature of democratic societies that results from citizens' free use of their practical reason.[160] However, instead of merely postulating or asserting this fact of reasonable pluralism, he also believed it important to seek an explanation for this feature about social life. He asks: "Why would free institutions with their basic rights and liberties lead to diversity? Why doesn't our sincere and conscientious attempt to

---

[158] For a comprehensive treatment of this transition, see Weithman (2012). Also see Freeman, Samuel. "Political Liberalism and the Possibility of a Just Democratic Constitution," in *Justice and the Social Contract*, Oxford University, 2007: 175-214.
[159] PL, xx.
[160] PL, xiv.

reason with one another lead us to agreement?"[161] These two questions "call for explanation."[162]

In answering these questions, Rawls first provides a few answers that are ultimately dismissed. He speculates that perhaps people are only motivated to hold views that "advance their own more narrow interests," and that because people have different interests, there would be different comprehensive views.[163] Next, he considers whether people are perhaps just too "irrational and not very bright," leading them to hopelessly confused thinking, creating multiple doctrines as a result.[164] Now, realists such as Elkins or Williams would presumably accept these explanations as sufficient to demonstrate the fact of disagreement—after all, people manifest these traits in various circumstances in politics in society all the time, so what is the problem? Aren't these traits widespread enough to base our political theories upon them? And yet, interestingly, Rawls rejects these explanations for reasonable pluralism, and it is important to examine the language that he uses in doing so. He says:

> These explanations are too easy, and not the kind we want. We want to know how reasonable disagreement is possible, *for we always begin work within ideal theory.* Thus, we ask: how might reasonable disagreement come about?[165]

Now, at first glance, this might sound like Rawls is just repeating the question without really clarifying what is wrong with the previous explanations of irrationality or narrowly

---

[161] JF, 35.
[162] Ibid., 35.
[163] Ibid., 35.
[164] Ibid., 35.
[165] Ibid., 35.

self-interested thinking. Yet, if we take his claim about ideal theory as providing a hint, we can construct a solution.

The main motivation for rejecting these kinds of explanations—and why we need ideal theory—is that such explanations do not represent a suitably general account of the person – they are, in a sense, based on a "nonideal" conception of the person. When Elkins describes persons as driven to subordinate others and to use political power to do so for their own narrow ends, there is no reason to believe, on Rawls's view, that such motives and impulses are *the central motives of our political lives*. They may, instead, simply be the result of disfigured and corrupted institutions in society; or, even if they may be genuine motives for us, they are not representative of our fundamental aims and pursuits.[166] As such, they cannot be used to explain the problem of disagreement in society. Hence, to avoid this problem, Rawls relies upon an "ideal conception of the person"[167] in order to isolate the core features of our moral personality and the central aspects of our political character.[168] We can then use this conception to demonstrate how disagreement is possible in a more fundamental way.

The essential components of the ideal conception of the person (later called the "political conception of the person" in *PL)* are related to how citizens in democratic life conceive of themselves, namely, as "free and equal," and having an interest in

---

[166] Rawls says: "We do not deny that vanity and greed, the will to dominate and the desire for glory are prominent in politics and affect the rise and fall of nations." Nevertheless, "we look for a political conception of justice that can gain the support of a reasonable overlapping consensus to serve as a public basis of justification," JF, 36-37.

[167] TJ, 231-232, later termed, the "political conception of the person," PL, 29-35.

[168] See Freeman, Samuel. *Rawls*. Routledge, 2007: 331.

developing the "two moral powers," which consist of (1) the capacity for a sense of justice—to recognize the constraints that fairness and reciprocity require—and (2) the capacity to revise and formulate a conception of the good.[169] These two capacities are directly related to what Rawls calls the "rational" and the "reasonable."[170] These notions all coalesce to provide a picture of a citizen who (1) has an interest in formulating and revising a conception of the good, (2) aims to advance her good in society while acknowledging that she must take responsibility for the ends she sets, and (3) strives to cooperate with others on terms of mutual respect and reciprocity.[171]

By providing an ideal conception of the person that represents our fundamental political aims, Rawls provides us with a conception of the person that is suitably *ideal* and *general* in the sense that "the deliberations of any one person are typical of all."[172] In basing the conception of the person on our liberal democratic culture, we can be

---

[169] See PL, 30-35.

[170] PL, 48-54.

[171] This is the interpretation advanced in *Political Liberalism* for the "political conception of the person." The alternative understanding of the "ideal conception of the person" as advanced in a *Theory of Justice* and "Kantian Constructivism" is based on the Kantian notion of full autonomy. Under that interpretation, we view ourselves as both morally and rationally autonomous. Our moral autonomy would be based upon the fact that humans can distinguish themselves as *acting for reasons* as opposed to merely following one's inclinations, and that these reasons must be justified to one another. The rational aspect of autonomy would be the fact that persons are not merely provided with ends—instead, persons formulate and critically evaluate their ends which determine their conception of the good and that they take whatever means they can to achieve it. Taken together, these capacities express the fundamental nature of *practical reasoning* itself. Rawls, in *PL*, gave up this more comprehensive justification for the reasonable and the rational aspects of the person and instead shifted to concepts that are politically available in democratic culture. See Freeman (2007): 284-323 for a further discussion of this transition.

[172] TJ, 232. However, "all" should be interpreted to mean "all persons in liberal democratic societies," not to all persons as such. On the Kantian interpretation of the conception of the person, Rawls would have argued that the "all" was much broader as the conception of the person was based on our fundamental practical reasoning, rather than simply a conception that is shared in liberal democratic societies.

assured that we are appealing to features of persons that are truly representative of citizens *qua* citizens.[173]

Broadly realist conceptions of the person, in contrast, do not accurately reflect our deepest aims and do not express our political personality. They are either too desolate and myopic—as reflected in the purely rational and self-interested person as represented by Hobbes—or they are too circumstantial—as reflected in the pessimistic realist who highlights the tendency for persons to use political power to subordinate others. Instead, Rawls believes that we conceive of ourselves as more than simply *homo economicus*, and that we have a far richer set of motives that enable us to cooperate with one another in liberal democratic life.

With the ideal conception of the person at hand, we can now return to our initial explanation of the fact of reasonable pluralism. Given that Rawls starts with an ideal conception of the person as free and equal with an interest in developing the two moral powers, we can now see how the normal activity of these persons in the course of democratic life will invariably generate a diversity of views that are permanent. In exercising the free use of their reason, citizens will come to recognize what Rawls calls the "burdens of judgement," which are the inherent limitations that citizens have in making judgments in conditions where there is incomplete information, complex

---

[173] Moreover, the ideal conception of the person is formulated in such a way such that we avoid a conception of the person that is grounded in a *perfectionist* ideal. Rawls believes that his task is "to define an ideal of the person without invoking a prior standard of human excellence", TJ, 287. Rawls does not believe that citizens acknowledging themselves as free and equal, or as having the two moral powers, is something that requires citizens to commit themselves to a unique comprehensive doctrine about the good, but is rather compatible with a plurality of reasonable conceptions of the good.

evidence, and differing methods for weighing values.[174] When citizens encounter these burdens over the course of their lives, they will naturally develop competing views about what should count as the good. More importantly, Rawls believes that our understanding of ourselves as free and equal—and as reasonable and rational—will prevent us from condoning the use of coercive state power to quash this pluralism. As Rawls states: "A continuing shared understanding on one comprehensive religious, philosophical, or moral doctrine can be maintained only by the oppressive use of state power."[175] It is "oppressive," for there would be no feasible way to remove disagreement about conceptions of the good from society without running afoul of our fundamental political aims that are central to the ideal conception of the person.[176]

We are now in a position to put all the pieces of the argument together and respond to the realist criticisms of Rawls. Rawls clearly recognizes the force of the objection by the realists that there cannot be unanimous (or near unanimous) agreement in a society characterized by deep disagreement. Rawls's account of the burdens of judgment and the ideal conception of the person guarantee that such disagreement will be a permanent feature of society. Moreover, Rawls believed that his understanding of reasonable pluralism caused him to revise his argument made in *A Theory of Justice*. Rawls states:

---

[174] For a complete account of the burdens of judgement, see PL, 54-58. Also JF, 35-36.

[175] PL, 37.

[176] In other words, we would not sacrifice our capacity to formulate a conception of the good with the hope that perhaps our own conception would be the one favored in our institutions. It is too great a risk to take and the cost of damaging one's fundamental powers would be too high.

> The fact of a plurality of reasonable but incompatible comprehensive doctrines...shows that, as used in *Theory*, the idea of a well-ordered society of justice as fairness is unrealistic. This is because it is inconsistent with realizing its own principles under the best of foreseeable conditions. The account of the stability of a well-ordered society is therefore also unrealistic and must be recast.[177]

From this statement, we can see that Rawls rejects the idea that it is feasible to expect citizens to converge on his unique conception of justice as fairness in society. Nevertheless, Rawls did not conclude that the best we could hope for was a *modus vivendi*, as realists would have us suppose.[178] Instead, in *Political Liberalism*, Rawls argues for the possibility of an "overlapping consensus" to emerge among a series of reasonable conceptions of the good that could find justification of political principles from within their own doctrines.[179] What would emerge is a "free-standing" political conception of justice that was independent of controversial metaphysical claims about the good, and could be endorsed from reasonable comprehensive views separately. Framed in this way, a Catholic, for instance, could accept justice as fairness by connecting it to God's notion of equality for all his creation; a Millian could endorse justice as fairness as the best way to promote individual autonomy; and a Kantian could accept it as the expression of ourselves as free and autonomous beings.

However, Rawls recognized the limits of this overlapping consensus, and eventually came to realize that an overlapping consensus on a *single* conception of justice—justice as fairness—was unlikely, and that it was only "a family of reasonable

---

[177] PL, xix.

[178] Rawls states that "it is not sufficient that [we] accept a democratic regime merely as a *modus vivendi*," PL, xxxix.

[179] PL, 133-168.

though differing liberal political conceptions" of justice that would be subject to an overlapping consensus (provided that such conceptions guaranteed the priority to the set of basic liberties and provided some guaranteed minimum all-purpose means).[180] Nevertheless, despite Rawls's own revisions to his theory, it is important to note that *these were not concessions to the external criticisms of realists.* This is evident in the fact that (1) Rawls never endorses *modus vivendi* liberalism and, that (2) Rawls offers a deep explanation for disagreement that does not rely upon a pessimistic or narrowly self-interested account of personhood. Instead, Rawls constructs an idealized conception of the person and proceeds to demonstrate how reasonable pluralism is possible from within that conception.

This should serve as a vindication of Rawls's ideal theory, for Rawls has established in the most general way possible that disagreement is both *possible and necessary* in democratic life by linking it with our most fundamental aims and the limiting facts of social life. Disagreement is not based upon a conception of human desires that is foreign to our considered judgments about ourselves and our aims. While Rawls undoubtedly recognizes our tendencies to dominate or subjugate others, he does not believe that these are the most representative of our own considered convictions about who we are as citizens in democracies. As such, any political conception of justice based upon a combative or domineering portrait of human agency

[180] PL, xxxviii. Rawls states that "the definition of liberal conceptions is given by three conditions: first, a specification of certain rights, liberties, and opportunities; second, a special priority for these freedoms; and third, measures assuring all citizens, whatever their social position, adequate all-purpose means to make intelligent and effective use of their liberties and opportunities, PL, xlviii. Rawls did hold, however, that justice as fairness was still the most reasonable.

will be unreasonable and unacceptable to us. In other words, a strongly realist conception of the person will not frame our understanding of the root causes of disagreement in society. If it did, we would have little reason to believe that *stable* agreements upon broadly liberal conceptions of justice could be possible. Any stability would be of momentary success and could only be maintained at great cost to our moral personality and our deepest aims. For Rawls, this would be a tragic outcome—one that is strongly at odds with his vision of a realistic utopia, for it would entail that the best we could hope for in society was a political conception of justice based largely upon external threats or mechanisms to keep our combative or self-serving desires in check. While Rawls does not disavow these sources of stability as impossible, Rawls's project is based upon the notion that we can *internally* accept and regard as reasonable our conception of justice. Otherwise, justice must be viewed as a foreign and oppressive force in our lives and not ultimately compatible with who we are as citizens. It would be difficult to "reconcile" ourselves to such a world in which justice could not be endorsed by citizens from within.[181]

---

[181] Rawls believes that one of the purposes of a realistic utopia is to "reconcile" ourselves to our social world. LP, 128. While Williams (2005) would object to this type of moralistic assessment of what persons are and what their fundamental aims should be, Rawls does not regard his theory as imposing a moral view upon persons at all, for Rawls believes that these features of ourselves can be represented to us in our deepest convictions in political society.

Chapter 4: A Reply to Amartya Sen

I. Introduction

We have already examined some realist criticisms of Rawls's methodology of ideal theory related to his assumption of full compliance and examined the problem of deep disagreement in society. However, other realists, such as Amartya Sen, have targeted different aspects of Rawls's ideal theory for criticism.[182] In particular, Sen has challenged the usefulness of the goal or target setting aspects of Rawls's ideal theory. Recall that, in addition to providing a methodology to test principles of justice against one another, Rawls aims to articulate an ideal of the perfectly just society—what Rawls calls the "well-ordered society"—in order to provide a formal model of what we should strive to achieve or aim for in our transition from nonideal circumstances to more ideal ones. The idea is that, by constructing a picture of the ideally just society, we can then make principled recommendations for improvement when faced with injustice by highlighting more urgent problems to address. For Rawls, it is only after we formulate the ideal can we can make genuine headway toward addressing injustice.

Sen rejects this model of the relationship between ideal theory and nonideal circumstances and advances the following thesis: an ideal theory of justice is *neither*

---

[182] Sen, Amartya. "What do we Want from a Theory of Justice?" *The Journal of Philosophy* vol. 53, no. 5 (2006): 215-238. Sen, Amartya. *The Idea of Justice*. Harvard University Press, 2009. For a sympathetic review of Sen's critique, see Schmidtz, David. "Nonideal Theory: What it is and What it Needs to Be," *Ethics* vol. 121, no. 4 (2011): 772-796. For an application and expansion of Sen's approach, see Wiens, David. "Prescribing Institutions Without Ideal Theory," *The Journal of Philosophy* vol. 20, no. 1 (2012): 45-70. For a criticism of Sen within a Rawlsian perspective, see Freeman, Samuel. "A New Theory of Justice," *The New York Review of Books*, October, 2010. For an expanded version of this criticism, see Freeman, Samuel. "Ideal Theory and the Justice of Institutions vs. Comprehensive Outcomes," *Rutgers Law Journal*, vol. 43, issue 2: 169-209.

necessary nor sufficient for addressing cases of actual injustice in the world.[183] While it may have other merits, providing us with guidance for correcting injustice is not one of them.[184] As such, Sen believes that political philosophers since Rawls have spent too much time articulating a vision of what the 'perfect,' 'pristine,' and 'spotlessly' just society would look like. Instead, Sen argues that a new way of thinking about justice is required for us to be able to address problems of the nonideal world.

Before we can address Sen's argument, we should provide a bit of vocabulary that Sen employs to characterize his objections. Sen characterizes theories of justice that focus on articulating the ideally organized society as "transcendental theories of justice."[185] These top-down approaches descend to the nonideal world only after fully articulating what the ideal society ought to be. That is, transcendental approaches do not begin to address the problems of the nonideal world—oppression, poverty, or lack of healthcare—until a full and complete conception of justice is outlined that relates all of the parts of justice together into one coherent whole.

In contrast, Sen's articulates an alternative approach to theorizing about justice, which he calls the "comparative" approach.[186] Central to this method is the idea that we are better off comparing two possible remedies of injustice against one another and evaluating which one enhances citizens' functionings better using tools from social

---

[183] Sen (2009): 15, "If a theory of justice is to guide reasoned choice of policies, strategies or institutions, then the identification of fully just social arrangements is neither necessary nor sufficient."
[184] Sen (2009): 101: "The search for [ideal justice] can be an engaging intellectual exercise in itself, but...it does not tell us much about the comparative merits of different societal arrangements.
[185] Sen (2006): 216.
[186] Ibid., 216-17.

choice theory and the capabilities approach to justice.[187] For instance, if our problem is poverty, we should select two concrete feasible proposals and do a pairwise analysis of the effects of these different systems on income and wealth distribution across society. Whichever model can produce better outcomes across the broad metric of the capabilities approach should be favored over the other. The aim of a comparative approach, then, is to outline the best method to rank and compare these alternatives in the real world, rather than wait until a total picture of justice is complete before we can begin to address injustice.

For Sen, the comparative model is superior to the transcendental model for several reasons, notably because it accurately reflects how we deliberate and argue for remedies to injustice in the actual political world. Sen's puts the point as such:

> The answers that a transcendental approach to justice gives—or can give—are quite distinct from the type of concerns that engage people in discussions on justice and injustice in the world, for example, iniquities of hunger, illiteracy, torture, arbitrary incarceration, or medical exclusion as particular social features that need remedying. The focus of these engagements tends to be on the ways and means of advancing justice—or reducing injustice—in the world by remedying these inequities, rather than on looking only for the simultaneous fulfilment of the entire cluster of perfectly just societal arrangements demanded by a particular transcendental theory.[188]

The problem, then, is that the transcendental approach is largely detached from the clamors for justice in the actual world and is largely powerless and inert in its efforts to address them. In essence, those who suffer from injustice must wait in abeyance until

---

[187] For a discussion of Sen's capabilities approach, see "Sen, Amartya, "Equality of What?" in *Tanner Lectures on Human Values*, ed. by Sterling McMurrin, Cambridge University Press, 1980. Also Sen, Amartya. *Development as Freedom*. New York: Knopf, 1999.
[188] Sen (2006): 218.

these timeless disputes about pristine justice are resolved once and for all before they can receive guidance about how to remedy the iniquities of the world. This model for thinking and theorizing about justice, according to Sen, should be unacceptable to us. Rather than devote precious intellectual capital constructing the ideal society, we should instead expend our efforts towards creating tools to evaluate proposals that offer incremental advantages over their predecessors. It is through this piecemeal approach to rectifying injustice can we genuinely impact the world and correct its numerous and diverse failures.

With this brief sketch of Sen's project in place, we can now outline the purposes of this section. First, I reconstruct Sen's argument that ideal theory is neither necessary nor sufficient for addressing problems of injustice. In doing so, I further buttress Sen's argument with a discussion of a well-known problem in economics known as the "problem of the second best." Next, I discuss in greater detail Sen's alternative "comparative approach" to justice. Finally, I respond to Sen's criticisms on behalf of Rawls, highlighting the importance of ideal theory for our thinking about justice even in nonideal circumstances.

II. Sen's Criticism of Rawls's Ideal Theory

Let us begin with Sen's statement of his thesis: "A transcendental approach is neither necessary nor sufficient for answering questions on the advancement of justice that urgently demand our attention, which call for a robustly comparative approach."[189]

---

[189] Ibid., 237.

The core of Sen's argument rests on a sufficiency claim and a necessity claim, which we will address in turn.

(a) Transcendental Justice is not *Sufficient* for Advancing Justice

According to Sen, a perfect theory of justice is not sufficient for enabling us to make successful judgements regarding the urgency or priority of injustices to be remedied. He states: "The identification of transcendence does not yield any means of addressing these problems to arrive at a relational ranking of departures from transcendence."[190] Sen provides an illuminating analogy to highlight this point: "The fact that a person regards the *Mona Lisa* as the best picture in the world does not reveal how she would rank a Gauguin against a Van Gogh."[191] She may think that it is the technique, color, and thematic ambiguity that, when combined, produce the ideal painting. However, given this information, we have little reason to think that we are now equipped with the tools that would be sufficient to compare other works of art against one another. Sure, we might be able to claim that all other works of art are "imperfect" for the simple reason that they *are not* the *Mona Lisa,* but we generally want more than this from a theory of aesthetics if we are going to make judgements between two imperfect works of art.

We can apply this analogy to the evaluation of societies with respect to justice. Sen argues that, just like our account of the perfect painting tells us nothing about how to rank and compare alternative paintings against one another, an account of the

---

[190] Sen (2009): 99.
[191] Sen (2006): 220, 221.

perfect society is inert with respect to our capacity to rank the desirability of feasible pairwise alternatives. We may, for instance, be able to describe the perfect society as one that realizes Rawls's two principles of justice, but this information is insufficient to provide guidance for how to rank nonideal alternatives that will vary in their failures across multiple dimensions with respect to their departures from the two principles of justice.

Suppose we have a society that violates multiple dimensions of the principle of liberty—citizens suffer, say, from both limited free speech and restricted freedom of religion. Or, citizens are both starving and do not have equal access to vote. In these cases, how are we to weigh these different competing concerns against one another? "Should we," Sen asks, "regard hunger, starvation and medical neglect to be invariably less important than the violation of any kind of personal liberty?"[192] Rawls's system, on Sen's account, simply labels these circumstances as "unjust."[193] As such, Sen argues that Rawls's theory is not helpful for addressing problems of actual injustice that societies face. We need a framework that is better equipped to handle the weighing of costs against one another. For these kinds of problems—those that involve weighing different alternatives— we require a "comparative" approach to thinking about justice that is designed specifically with a system for evaluating these kinds of trade-offs.

[192] Sen (2009): 65.

[193] Even Rawls's priority of liberty, Sen argues, is too vague to aid us with these difficult questions. I will return to a discussion of this point later in the chapter.

(b) An Illustration of the Sufficiency Objection: The Problem of the Second Best

One way to expand upon Sen's general objection to the transcendental approach is to compare it with a well-known problem in economics which has received some attention: the problem of the second best.[194] First introduced by economists R.G. Lipsey and Kelvin Lancaster, the central problem contains two logically related claims. The first asserts that:

> The general theorem for the second best optimum states that if there is introduced into a general equilibrium system a constraint which prevents the attainment of one of the Paretian conditions, the other Paretian conditions, although still attainable, are, in general, no longer desirable.[195]

The second, corollary claim is as follows:

> There is no *a priori* way to judge as between various situations in which some of the Paretian optimum conditions are fulfilled while others are not. Specifically, it is *not* true that a situation in which more, but not all, of the optimum conditions are fulfilled is necessarily, or is even likely to be, superior to a situation in which fewer are fulfilled.[196]

The general idea is that, if we have a list of conditions that are part of the ideal, it is not necessarily the case that, if one those features is missing, the other features will still be desirable. We can illustrate the problem using a familiar example. Suppose I believe that the ideal cookie is a cookie that has chocolate chips and pecans. Now, we can ask the question, do we have *sufficient* information to be able to determine what the

---

[194] Lipsey, R.G. and Kelvin Lancaster. "The General Theory of Second Best." *The Review of Economic Studies*, Vol. 24, No. 1, 1956-57: 11-32. Robert Goodin has also discussed this in his criticism of political idealism. See Goodin, Robert. "Political Ideals and Political Practice," *British Journal of Political Science* 25 (1995): 37-56.

[195] Ibid., 11.

[196] Ibid., 12.

second-best, third-best, and fourth-best cookies are? In other words, are we able to rank cookies that are nonideal? The general tendency is to assume that the second-best cookie should have some of the elements of the ideal cookie—surely it will have chocolate chips! However, according to this theorem—and Sen's sufficiency objection—this is not necessarily true. In fact, the second-best cookie may simply be a macadamia nut cookie, and may have nothing to do with chocolate chips or pecans.[197]

Using this analogy, Harvard economist, Dani Rodrik invoked the general theory of the second best to criticize proponents of *laissez-faire* capitalism and to argue in favor of government-controlled markets.[198] Adherents to the *laissez-faire* approach would generally condemn any form of governmental market regulation. The rationale was that, since unrestricted free markets were the ideal and most efficient model, any governmental regulation would take us further away from our realization of it and must therefore be worse.

However, Rodrik's reply to these economists was to invoke the problem of the second best. He argued that the second-best solution for us may have little in common with the unrestricted market, and instead, rigorously controlled markets by the government could be second-best.

---

[197] Similarly, the third best may be a snickerdoodle cookie, while fourth best, a regular chocolate chip cookie.

[198] Rodrik, Dani. "Why do economists disagree?" http://rodrik.typepad.com/dani_rodriks_weblog/2007/08/why-do-economis.html (2007, August 5th). For a rebuttal, see Free Exchange, "Making the second best of it," *The Economist*, http://www.economist.com/node/20015054/print (2007, August 21st).

Bringing the analogy to bear on our current topic, we can apply this reasoning to the limitations of transcendental theories of justice. The argument would be that Rawls's ideal of the well-ordered society governed by the two principles of justice is not sufficient to inform us how to rank alternatives that are nonideal. For, while it may be tempting to think that the second-best society would be a kind of gradual and mixed realization of Rawls's two principles of justice, it may be the case that it is actually a utilitarian society, while the third best would be a libertarian society.

Moreover, this can have important implications when attempting to determine how we should improve our current state of affairs. After all, if it turns out that the next best thing for us is a utilitarian society, then it would be a serious mistake to employ Rawls's ideal of a well-ordered society to instantly condemn proposals aimed at maximizing average utility in society if the ideal was not currently a feasible alternative for us. If we return to the cookie analogy, we might say that it would be improper to condemn the chef for buying macadamia nuts instead of chocolate chips, if it turned out there were no pecans.

Of course, these are mere speculations regarding what the second-best or third-best societies would be for us. The important point, however, is that the problem of the second best cannot be solved "*a priori*," as Lipsey and Lancaster claim. We cannot read off from the well-ordered society how to determine the next best course of action when the ideal is unavailable. Instead, we require an additional framework to handle these kinds of assessments.

To put it back in Sen's terminology, the ideal of transcendental justice would not be *sufficient* to provide us guidance in nonideal circumstances. We require a "comparative" approach to justice in order to identify proposals that would enhance justice in society from a worse state of affairs to a better one.

(c) Transcendental Theories are not *Necessary* for Advancing Justice

In addition to claiming that transcendental theories of justice are not *sufficient* for correcting injustice, Sen also argues that they are not *necessary* for it either. Sen illustrates this objection with a compelling example:

> Mount Everest is the tallest mountain in the world, completely unbeatable in terms of stature by any other peak, but that understanding is neither needed, nor particularly helpful, in comparing the peak heights of, say, Mount Kilimanjaro and Mount McKinley. There would be something very deeply odd in a general belief that a comparison of any two alternatives cannot be sensibly made without a prior identification of a supreme alternative. There is no analytical connection there at all.[199]

Here, Sen illustrates that we do not require an ideal model—Mount Everest is the highest mountain—in order to make pairwise comparisons between two alternatives—Mount Kilimanjaro is taller than Mount McKinley. If we apply this analogy to the case of justice, the claim would be that we do not require a picture of Rawls's perfect well-ordered society in order to assert the injustice of, say, global poverty and widespread illiteracy and advocate for concrete, piecemeal improvements in any of these metrics. Indeed, on Sen's reasoning, it would be absurd to claim that, unless we knew what perfect justice required, we could not advocate for health policies designed to alleviate

---

[199] Sen (2009): 102. Also quoted in Sen (2006): 222.

serious global illnesses, or proposals to provide education to women in developing countries. For Sen, we already have agreement about these problems in order to establish a priority in addressing them. There is no necessity to search for the perfect society to make progress in these initiatives.

Framed in this way, Sen is highlighting the irrelevance of ideal theory if we are interested in advancing justice and eliminating injustice in society. There is no "analytical connection" between recognizing the benefits of providing healthcare to poor families and the picture of the perfect society governed by Rawls's two principles of justice. As such, we would be wasting our efforts debating the intricacies of Rawls's pristine theory of justice when real work could be done employing a comparative approach to justice that would be designed to better implement and justify workable improvements to our deeply unjust world.

(d) Do Comparative Theories entail Transcendental Theories?

Sen immediately foresees a potential counterargument to his position, namely, that the ability to make pairwise comparisons must entail the ability to identify a transcendental ideal. Or, as Sen puts it, "if comparative assessments can be systematically made, then that discipline must also be able to identify the very best."[200] The intuition here is that, surely if we can compare the height of two mountains, we have enough information to be able to determine what the highest mountain is.

---

[200] Ibid., 222.

However, Sen argues that this is a *"non sequitur."*[201] It does not follow that "a sequence of pairwise comparisons invariably leads us to the very best."[202] Instead, the exercise only permits the identification of better alternatives, *as the very best may not exist at all.* For instance, in the case of mountains, just because we can compare the relative heights of two peaks does not tell us anything about Mount Everest—its height, its location, or whether it even exists. To emphasize this point, Sen points out that our set comparisons will inevitably be incomplete—it is impossible that we will be able to generate a total set of all possibilities to compare. So there is no reason to think that our ability to make comparisons in one—or any finite number of situations—will entail our capacity to identify or locate the very best.

In this regard, Sen's account of justice is fundamentally open-ended—a never-ending task of incremental improvements with the hope that our gravest injustices in the world will eventually be eliminated. Whether or not we ultimately converge on some perfect society is neither here nor there for these purposes. In fact, to attempt such a task would be an irrelevant distraction that would hamper our capacity to solve concrete and identifiable problems that demand rectification.

(e) Judgments of Justice are Always Incomplete

In addition to being more open-ended, Sen admits that the comparative method he advances may not always yield *definitive* judgments to questions about which proposal would be better than another. There will always be an essential

---

[201] Sen (2009): 102.
[202] Sen (2006): 223.

"incompleteness" regarding a proposal's effectiveness in advancing justice. The reasons for this, according to Sen, are as follows: "Incompleteness may be of the lasting kind for several reasons, including unbridgeable gaps in information, and judgmental unresolvability involving disparate considerations that cannot be entirely eliminated, even with full information.[203] Given these problems that are endemic to practical judgement, he admits that the comparative approach will never produce full or "totalist" principles that provide "complete" answers.[204]

However, Sen does not view this as a fault within comparative theories. Instead, Sen believes that we can still arrive at reasonable decisions that will eliminate injustice, even in the face of indeterminacy. For example, using the comparative approach, we could strongly denounce "endemic hunger or exclusion from medical access" despite "durable incompleteness" regarding the inability to determine whether or not the *ideal* tax rate in the highest bracket is 45% or 46%.[205] We could easily set that question aside while still making headway in advancing justice in society. Put more starkly in contrast to Rawls, we need not determine which given tax scheme *best* comports with the difference principle if we have sufficient data and evidence to increase taxes to address major violations of justice. To get bogged down by *that* indeterminacy would paralyze us, rendering our theory of justice inert.[206] In contrast to Rawls, Sen claims: "The challenge of assessing *advancement*, or identifying *regression*, will very often be not

---

[203] Ibid., 223. These appear similar to Rawls's "burdens of judgment," PL, 54-58. Also JF, 35-36.
[204] Ibid., 223.
[205] Ibid., 223-224.
[206] For a similar objection, see Farrelly, Colin. "Justice in Ideal Theory: A Refutation," *Political Studies* 55 (2007): 844-64.

compromised at all by the presence of substantial incompleteness in the rankings of justice."[207]

(f) What do we Want from a Theory of Justice?

Given these various objections to transcendental approaches, Sen asks us to reframe our thinking of the very idea of justice:

> The question "What is a just society?" is not a good *starting point* for a useful theory of justice. To that has to be added the further conclusion that it may not be a plausible *end point* either. A systematic theory of comparative justice does not need, nor does it necessarily yield, an answer to the question "What is a just society?[208]

For Sen, asking "What is a just society?" will never yield answers on its own to what we should do to promote justice in our world. Instead, Sen believes that we would be better off asking a different kind of question, perhaps such as, "How can we reasonably advance justice in society?" This would involve assessing the current state of affairs, and comparing it with a feasible alternative. So long as it produces an improvement from the previous state, we can be assured that we have eliminated injustice and done the best we can in improving our world.

(g) Sen's Comparative Approach

Through Sen's criticisms of Rawls, we have briefly suggested at some of the goals that the comparative approach to justice should accomplish. Most importantly, it should enable us to weigh alternatives in a clearer and more precise manner than Rawls's transcendental approach without requiring us to provide a complete answer to

---

[207] Sen (2006): 237.
[208] Ibid., 226. Also see Sen (2009): 105.

the question: "what is the just society?" Sen develops this proposal in greater detail through his more extensive work, *The Idea of Justice*.[209]

Briefly, Sen advocates for an approach that combines elements of social choice theory, a capabilities approach as the relevant metric of justice, consequentialism, public reasoning, and a theory of impartiality that is related to Adam Smith's account of an impartial spectator.[210] The general idea is this: When deliberating about various social policies in the public forum, we should imagine ourselves as an impartial spectator who is charged with adopting the preferences of all. Our aim should be to maximize the capabilities for functioning for citizens, suitably constrained by considerations of individual rights and fairness.[211] We are then to assess which proposal would best satisfy these considerations.

As Sen warns, the comparative approach outlined requires a great deal of knowledge about social choice theory, mathematical modelling, and empirical analysis—tools that philosophers have little expertise in.[212] Social choice theory generally specializes in determining what the best choice for society should be when preferences and values among people are vastly different. A great deal of literature spans this

---

[209] Sen (2009).

[210] See Freeman (2010): 5.

[211] Sen's account of consequentialism is a mixed conception in the sense that it is not simply happiness or pleasure that it is maximized, but rather the entire bundle of considerations which include capabilities, fairness, rights, justice, etc. For a criticism of the dangers of bundling together deontological considerations into a consequential framework see Freeman (2006): 80-90.

[212] According to Sen: "The comparative approach is central to the analytical discipline of 'social choice theory'....The literature of social choice theory is typically quite technical and largely mathematical, and since many of the results in the field cannot be established except through fairly extensive mathematical reasoning, its basic approach has received relatively little attention, especially from philosophers," Sen (2009): 17-18.

subject regarding the best model to use, especially given the influential results of Arrow's impossibility theorem, which states that we cannot have a choice procedure that is both rational and democratic that successfully translates individual preferences of citizens into a clear social preference.[213] Nevertheless, Sen believes that his comparative approach is best equipped to address these interdisciplinary problems.

III. Reply to Sen

While Sen provides some powerful points regarding the limitations of ideal theory, and presents an interesting alternative to thinking about justice in a comparative framework, many of his criticisms fail to adequately establish the claim that we should abandon ideal theory and transcendental theories of justice. In this reply, I will first address Sen's claim that ideal theory is neither necessary nor sufficient for advancing justice in society. Next, I will evaluate Sen's own comparative approach to justice and argue that his own proposal does not adequately solve the problems he believes beset Rawls's own model. Finally, I will respond to Sen's claim that ideal theory is a distraction form more pressing concerns of injustice.

(a) Is the Ideal Sufficient?

According to Sen's sufficiency argument, Rawls's principles of justice cannot, by themselves, accurately assess varying departures from the ideal model, nor provide a rank ordering between alternatives. Only a comparative approach to justice can do this. Now, strictly speaking, Rawls denies this, for he believes that the lexical priority of the

---

[213] Arrow, Kenneth. *Social Choice and Individual Values*, Yale University Press, 1951.

principles establishes which departures from the ideal are more urgent to address.[214] For instance, when faced with a situation in which we must choose between protecting liberty or promoting equality of opportunity, we should favor establishing the equal basic liberties. However, Sen rejects this reply and argues that such recommendations can lead to a form of "extremism" that can be at odds with the empirical realities of the world.[215]

However, Rawls does recognize that the lexical priority rule can admit exceptions, so the accusation of "rule-worship" is misplaced. Rawls states: "To accept the lexical ordering of the two principles, we are not forced to deny that the feasibility of the basic liberties depends upon circumstances."[216] For instance, a situation in which people lacked sufficient resources to even exercise the basic liberties would clearly be a case where the lexical priority would not hold. Rawls says:

> This principle [of liberty] may be preceded by a lexically prior principle requiring that basic needs be met, at least insofar as their being met is a necessary condition for citizens to understand and to be able fruitfully to exercise the basic rights and liberties.[217]

So, to answer Sen's supposedly rhetorical question, "Why should we regard hunger, starvation and medical neglect to be invariably less important than the violation of any kind of personal liberty?," our answer is that we shouldn't, and Rawls does not commit us to the view that we should.[218] If the basic needs of citizens are not met—if citizens

---

[214] TJ, 216.
[215] Sen (2009): 59. Sen also states that "total unrestrained priority is almost certainly an overkill," 65.
[216] TJ, 217-18.
[217] JF, 44, fn. 7.
[218] Sen (2009): 65.

are facing starvation—the relief of such circumstances will be lexically prior the basic liberties insofar as rectifying those problems ensures that the basic needs can eventually be restored.

Sen is still critical, however, that Rawls's theory does not do more than this. It does not, for instance, provide us with precise ways of weighing different basic liberties against one another, other than to ensure that we have "a fully adequate scheme of equal basic liberties."[219] But Rawls thinks that it is inappropriate for fundamental principles of justice to admit of such precision. Rawls says that it is a mistake to "think a political conception should be framed to cover all logically possible cases, or all conceivable cases."[220] This is because these basic principles of justice require *interpretation* as part of the "four-stage sequence" of application for principles to society.[221] For instance, according to Rawls, the principle of liberty "applies not only to the basic structure but more specifically to what we think of as the constitution."[222] As is well known, constitutional principles such as the Equal Protection Clause or the freedom of the press can develop into a numerous array of implications for citizens that are not known *a priori* from Rawls's first principle of justice. As such, it would be too demanding and unrealistic to expect constitutional principles to settle all disputes without any further interpretation at a later stage in application of those principles—either judicial or legislative. Sen, in other words, is simply asking for too much for our

---

[219] JF, 42.
[220] JF, 43, fn. 5.
[221] For a discussion of Rawls's "four-stage sequence" in applying his principles of justice. See JF, 48; PL, 397-98; TJ, 171-176.
[222] JF, 46.

most abstract expressions of the standards of justice for society. These principles will eventually be applied to address the concerns that Sen is rightfully concerned about during the application stage of these principles.

Given Rawls's more limited aims, it is doubtful that Rawls believed that his ideal theory on its own could accomplish any more than a general structure of our priorities and our goals. Rawls plainly admits that much needs to be filled in when applying an ideal theory of justice to the circumstances of the real world:

> As far as circumstances permit, we have a natural duty to remove any injustices, beginning with the most grievous as identified by the extent of the deviation from perfect justice. Of course, *this idea is extremely rough. The measure of departures from the ideal is left importantly to intuition.* [223]

While Rawls says that "intuition" will be required to supply additional normative tools to the analysis, he does not mean that we will not be required to consult the social sciences to determine the costs and consequences of various proposals, or to determine the feasibility and likelihood of success for each correction of injustice. As Simmons points out in his explication of Rawls, "nonideal theory will require judgments of both philosophical and social-scientific sorts."[224] So Rawls is actually in agreement with Sen regarding the insufficiency for ideal theory to provide us with a *complete* roadmap with respect to addressing departures from the ideal.

However, where Rawls and Sen differ is with respect to whether Rawls's picture is sufficiently able to provide *any* guidance with respect to assessing and correcting

---

[223] TJ, 216, emphasis added.
[224] Simmons (2010): 19.

injustice. As we have just explored, an odd implication of Sen's criticism here is that it calls into question the purpose of all constitutional documents that contain general abstract principles, as Samuel Freeman notes.[225] Sen's position appears to lead to the striking conclusion that foundational documents that outline broad principles for society are pointless for advancing justice. As such, Sen's criticisms are too strong and lead to an unwarranted suspicion of the relevance of the background principles that structure our own society.

Let us now return to Sen's analogy comparing famous works of art which he relies upon to illustrate his criticisms. Recall that Sen asserts that our knowledge that the *Mona Lisa* is the best painting cannot provide us with any information regarding how to rank a Van Gogh versus a Gauguin. However, this simplified analogy is misleading, and, upon further examination, it misses crucial aspects of our identification of the ideal. To illustrate, if we are only provided with the minimal claim that "The *Mona Lisa* is the best painting," we will of course not have learned much. However, once we probe more deeply into the *reasons why* we believe the *Mona Lisa* is the best painting, we will certainly have a basis for evaluating other nonideal paintings.[226] For instance, if asked to justify the preference for the *Mona Lisa,* we will presumably uncover something about the importance of theme, style, and technique and how those elements shape our understanding of art. It would be quite strange indeed if these

---

[225] See Freeman (2010): 6.

[226] Also see Swift, Adam. "The Value of Philosophy in Nonideal Circumstances," *Social Theory and Practice* 34, 2008: 372-75. Also see Goodin (1995): 45: "Problems of second best arise particularly when descriptions are couched in terms of surface attributes rather than more directly in terms of the underlying sources of those values."

values had no relevance to our evaluation of other imperfect paintings. After all, how would it make sense for our judgements about style or technique to simply disappear from our assessments of other paintings? It is simply not possible for these evaluative elements to drop out of our comparison of nonideal paintings.

Similarly, we can apply this reasoning to address the "problem of the second best" illustrated by economists. If we return to the analogy with the cookie, it is clear that, once we uncover the reasons why we believe the chocolate chip and pecan cookie to be the best, we can draw upon those explanations to see why the macadamia cookie would be second-best. The lesson of the "problem of the second best" is, therefore, only the following: We should not rely on *surface attributes* for determining which properties the second or third-best solutions will have.[227] Of course the second-best cookie might not have chocolate chips. The chocolate chips are just a façade for the deeper rationale for why that cookie is best. Once we shift to our knowledge of the value judgments and evaluative comparisons, the problem disappears. Our intimate knowledge of these more fundamental elements will always be applicable to whatever nonideal element we are analyzing.

Let us provide a more dramatic example to illustrate this point. Suppose you knew which cookie was the ideal cookie *and you knew why*. What follows from this? You would have to know everything important about cooking and about all the ingredients, and all the values associated with weighing different styles of cooking.

---

[227] Goodin (1995): 45 uses the language of "surface attributes."

Otherwise, how could you have identified the ideal? Surely, if you could do this, you would know how to rank nonideal cookies against one another, as well as identify the second and third best. In fact, *pace* Sen, you would be able to establish a complete rank ordering of them.

Now, we might object and say that I have proved too much with this example. For we then may wonder, how can Rawls truly establish the ideally just society? Does Rawls know everything about all possible societies and all possible elements? Surely not. However, this does not weaken my argument, for two main reasons: (1) Rawls limits the scope of his investigation and (2) Rawls does not view the "ideal society" in the same way we might think of an ideal cookie.

With respect to (1), Rawls is not interested in the ideally just society for all possible worlds and all possible people.[228] Instead, Rawls limits his inquiry to liberal democratic societies under the circumstances of justice and favorable conditions, and to human beings who regard themselves as free and equal and are subject to human constraints. Nor does Rawls allow deliberators all possible conceptions of justice when determining which principles should govern society. Rather, he presents them a list of various conceptions that have currency in the political culture.[229] This should already simplify a great deal the conditions under which an ideal is identified.

With respect to (2), Rawls does not think that identifying an ideal society is about *maximizing* something in the way we might think that an ideal cookie somehow

---

[228] TJ, 137-138.
[229] TJ, 105-106.

maximizes pleasure, or how an ideal form of travel maximizes speed. We greatly misunderstand Rawls if we think his vision of an ideally just society somehow mirrors these other kinds of 'ideal' conceptions that aim to maximize. Instead, Rawls believes that an ideal society is one that is identified by principles that we believe to be the most *reasonable* for us given certain specified conditions. They are most reasonable not because they are shown to maximize something or abide by some comprehensive doctrine of perfection, but rather because they answer to our deepest considered convictions implicit in our liberal democratic culture and are capable of being agreed upon by citizens who regard themselves as free and equal.

It is within *this* defined context that Rawls identifies an ideally just society. And within this context, Rawls does believe to have best incorporated all the different considered convictions (the "cooking ingredients") into one ideal vision that each citizen can individually acknowledge to be the ideal. What follows is that, given our intimate understanding of the various components that determine our selection of the principles of justice, we should be able to have sufficient knowledge to judge at least the broad framework for ranking nonideal alternatives and identifying second or third best societies. Put in another way, through the process of identifying the ideally just society, each citizen would know much more than just the two principles of justice. In fact, each citizen would understand the deep reasons that inform the basis for them—the social basis of self-respect, the importance of reciprocity, the importance of our conception of the good and having the primary goods to pursue it, and the relevance of justification to others that can be seen as reasonable. Each of these elements will be deeply connected in the normative outlook of persons in society, and it would be shocking if these substantive commitments could not serve as a wellspring of ideas for how to assess nonideal conditions in the world. Yes, we will be left with "intuition" in some cases as Rawls reminds us,[230] but this is not because his ideal theory is *silent* with respect to the nonideal world, but rather because no one can work out a theory for each and every possible circumstance. This is not possible given the nature and complexity of the world. And yet, the tools that have been gained through the process of identifying the ideal will be invaluable and will greatly aid citizens in providing solutions and navigating us toward justice.[231]

(b) Is the Ideal Necessary?

Next, we can move to the claim that transcendental theories of justice are not *necessary* for advancing justice in nonideal circumstances. Recall that Sen employs the analogy with Mount Everest and denies its relevance for making pairwise comparisons between two other mountains in terms of their height. He then applies this reasoning to ideal theories of justice, denying that they are necessary to identify and compare the injustices of global malnutrition, gender discrimination in education, and other urgent problems of our world. On the surface, this makes intuitive sense. It seems odd to require the identification of the ideal to be able to make a judgement between two

---

[230] TJ, 216.

[231] This exposition also nicely illustrates the importance and benefits of the *publicity condition* for a theory of justice. If principles and their full justification are available to citizens, then the citizens will be better equipped to handle nonideal theory, for they will have individual access to the deep connections between their own considered convictions and the world around them.

societies with varying degrees of illiteracy. Nevertheless, the analogy has significant limitations when we examine its implications more carefully.

To begin, Simmons offers a response to Sen, arguing that we require the identification of the ideal so as to provide a broader viewpoint from which to gauge our piecemeal improvements. Simmons states: "To dive into nonideal theory without an ideal theory in hand is simply to drive blind, to allow irrational free rein to the mere conviction of injustice and to eagerness for change of any sort."[232] Simmons warns us that, under Sen's approach, using a comparative approach is short-sighted and may only lead to a temporary improvement to a situation, without actually leading us toward the peak of justice. To illustrate, if I am trying to build a better car, I can make several piecemeal improvements to the interior before realizing that, all along, I was making it harder and harder to leave enough room for the engine. As such, we need a broader picture of the blueprint before making improvements, which is what ideal theory seeks to achieve.

Of course, Sen can reply that all considerations should be taken into account when making improvements, so it would be unlikely that we would ever fail to leave enough room for an engine. However, the objection still stands: there is no reason to think that we are properly weighing all the considerations until we have a long-term plan or goal. For instance, without a broader picture of the goals of car-building, we might never accurately weigh the consideration for energy efficiency—it might simply

[232] Simmons (2010): 34.

be dropped out or dwarfed by other considerations of car design and so never get implemented. Moreover, this outcome is compatible with making constant piecemeal improvements to the car every year.

However, I believe we can strengthen Simmons's point in a more robust manner than he has presented. It is not simply the danger that we are "driving blind" without ideal theory. Even more importantly, it is not clear that any piecemeal improvements we make *will last* without ideal theory. Recall the importance of the stability condition that Rawls builds into his theory of justice, which requires that our principles gain the internal support of citizens through reliable psychological mechanisms. By utilizing ideal theory, we are better able to test for which kinds of principles will genuinely garner the support of citizens so that they carry well into the future. Without ideal theory, it is not clear whether a given short-term improvement we make will not simply vanish in vain. This can be a very costly oversight, for we may be directed on a comparative approach to justice to make small improvements to literacy or poverty with no basis upon which to think that such incremental advantages will pass on to future generations. Without the lasting institutional structural changes regulated by principles of justice that *can be endorsed by citizens*, we run the risk of sabotaging our noble, but short-sighted efforts. As such, the stability condition that is offered by ideal theory should be viewed as *necessary* for our work in nonideal theory. Sen's comparative approach, by contrast, does not adequately incorporate the stability condition on proposed solutions, and so there is no reliable method to make lasting change.[233]

(c) Does the Ideal Even Exist?

We can now turn to a more radical objection to what I have proposed in defense of ideal theory. According to David Schmidtz, these kinds of responses miss an important element of Sen's objections.[234] According to Schmidtz, "justice has no peak form. For thousands of years we postulated that it did, but we never had any reason, and we were wrong....Justice is not a place we need to get to."[235] For Schmidtz, there is no transcendental ideal theory of justice, so there is no reason to attempt to describe it or assume it would be helpful to us. Instead, the most important task for us is to get out of "pits" of injustice and avoid them in the future as best we can.[236] Hence, the only model available to us is the comparative approach to justice.

Schmitdz's more skeptical conclusion about justice demands a fuller treatment than I can provide here, but I will provide one major point to consider. We should remember that, for Rawls, when he describes an ideal theory of justice, he is not describing something like the tallest mountain, the perfect car, or a society governed by a comprehensive doctrine of the good. Rawls would agree that *this* kind of ideally just

---

[233] We might object and say that stability can simply be added into the calculus to be maximized with all the other considerations. But this misses the force of this objection. *A comparative approach to justice cannot truly identify what counts as a genuinely stable solution.* Ideal theory is the best tool to determine which kinds of solutions will ultimately last.
[234] Schmidtz (2011): 775.
[235] Ibid., 774.
[236] Ibid., 774. Schmidtz of course does not mean that justice does not exist; rather, he means that there is no perfectly just society for us to describe. Justice simply identifies wrongs and tells us to steer clear from them when making improvements.

society would be impossible. In contrast, however, Rawls is articulating a society that is governed by *the most reasonable principles* given certain limitations and circumstances in political life that Rawls believes can be subject to an overlapping consensus.

Framed in this manner, we must understand Schmidtz's objection as amounting to the claim that there simply are no principles of justice that all reasonable persons can accept. However, this might seem to leave us with a bit of a puzzle then, for what is the status of Sen's comparative *theory of justice*? Surely, it advocates for principles that people should agree upon. For instance, the comparative approach says the following: "We ought to adopt an impartial spectator to rank-order different states of affairs by aggregating all considerations of capabilities, rights, liberties, well-being, costs, etc." All societies that fail to do this would be unjust. Doesn't Schmidtz's skepticism apply to Sen's approach as well?

However, this would mischaracterize the comparative approach to justice, for the recommendation to adopt the perspective of an impartial spectator, coupled with a pluralistic account of goods to be maximized, *is not justice*, but is the *method for best realizing justice*. For Sen, *justice is about realizing states-of-affairs* in society that we can construct methods to help us achieve. In this sense, justice would be identified with a concrete outcome such as achieving certain capabilities for freedom, literacy, health, opportunity and a level of income. Anyone in society would be able to *see* and *witness* justice being done, for they would be able to assess the freedoms and capabilities of citizens increasing around them.

In reply, this is not how Rawls conceives of justice, and it highlights the deep chasm that exists between "contractarian deontological"[237] and consequentialist approaches to political theorizing. Rawls does not think justice is fundamentally about maximizing or aggregating anything, or evaluating states of affairs independent of social institutions, even if those states of affairs involve thriving and flourishing persons. Such states-of-affairs *may realize other values that are important*, but we cannot evaluate *justice* from merely looking at how people's lives are going.

Instead, for Rawls, justice is about selecting principles to govern social institutions that reasonable persons who regard themselves as free and equal can agree upon, provided that these principles take their higher-order interests seriously and attempt to fairly distribute the goods that they jointly produce. Absent these deeply social conditions between persons, justice cannot have any application or render any verdict.

Of course, it is this very understanding of justice that Schmidtz and Sen seek to reject and replace, as they believe that it is too limited in scope and unnecessarily complicates our commonsense judgments about justice. After all, why can't we simply regard the malnourishment of persons in the world as a grave injustice that demands rectification? Why isn't the widespread subjection of women simply a fact of injustice, regardless of its social origins?

---

[237] Rawls's view can be characterized as "contractarian deontological." See Alexander, Larry. "Deontological Ethics," *Stanford Encyclopedia of Philosophy* https://plato.stanford.edu/entries/ethics-deontological/#ConDeoThe [2016, Oct. 17th].

Rawls's response here of course would be to admit that these are deep problems with the world, and that many of them are, in fact, injustices. However, Rawls would also urge us to separate *humanitarian urgencies* from *grave injustices.*[238] The duties to rectify these problems will take a different shape and fall on different agents who are responsible for correcting them depending upon the ultimate source of these horrible states-of-affairs. This will involve a complex set of considerations involving capability to aid, responsibility for harm, and institutional failings, etc. I cannot develop a comprehensive account of these considerations here, but it is important to emphasize that distributive justice is a *unique* responsibility that is owed to persons in virtue of the institutional and social relationships that exist between them, and that a consequentialist or comparative approach to justice will fail to capture this important normative difference in their proposed solutions to these problems.

Returning to the challenge at hand, even *if* Schmidtz and Sen agreed that Rawls's understanding of justice offered an important insight on the relevance of social relationships for justice, it still would not settle the deeper objection that *agreement is not ultimately possible* in Rawls's model, despite all its other virtues. However, I believe that this is mistaken. To be sure, Rawls recognizes at the later stages of his life that agreement would only be possible on a family of liberal conceptions of justice, so Rawls only needs to defend the weaker objection that even a more modest overlapping

[238] He would also urge us to make a distinction between the duties of global justice which include the duty to aid "burdened societies" from the duties of distributive justice. See LP, 37.

consensus would be impossible.[239] However, as I do not have the space to address that more fundamental challenge here, I will instead end this section with a different reply to Schmidtz's challenge.

To deny, as Schmidtz does, that there is an ideal of justice at all is really to say that there are no ideal conceptions that are possible at all in our thinking—only recommendations that tell us of better or worse ways of doing things. It would be akin to saying, there is no ideal of friendship—no principles that describe its ultimate shape. Instead, there are only better or worse ways of being a friend. Or, it would amount to claiming that truth is not a governing principle for the relations between persons. Instead, there would only be better or worse ways of conveying information with each other.

This more radical approach to our normative theorizing demands a more comprehensive reply than I can provide here, but it is important nonetheless to see how significantly it departs from our normative thinking in these matters.

(d) Sen's Comparative Approach

Setting aside Schmidtz's criticisms of ideal theory, we can now evaluate the success of Sen's comparative approach to justice on its own merits. Recall that Sen believes the comparative approach to justice is better equipped to remedy injustice in the world for it allows us to rank states of affairs against one another and suggests immediate correction of an injustice. It does so by recommending that we adopt an

---

[239] PL, xxxviii.

impartial spectator that asks us to aggregate capabilities for functioning, along with rights and liberties and concerns for fairness. These capabilities for functioning are the resources, opportunities and tools necessary for citizens to achieve the conditions of freedom.[240] However, what makes Sen's approach distinct is his bundling together of deontological considerations with consequentialist ones. He does so because he recognizes the plurality of goods that people seek, and wants to safeguard the rights and liberties of others if maximization of another metric threatens them.

However, according to Freeman, this kind of reformulation is "ad hoc" and "risks sacrificing traditional strengths of utilitarianism by obscuring the practical consequences of his view."[241] One of the virtues of traditional utilitarianism is that it is able to provide a clear metric for weighing conflicts against one another. But once we attempt to factor in deontological elements such as rights and fairness, it will be more difficult to resolve the tensions between the different components.[242] It is unclear, for instance, how we are to weigh the capabilities for freedom for some at the expense of procedural fairness for others.

In reply, Sen admits that there is some invariable "incompleteness" to his account. However, he argues that it is not problematic, for we can sometimes sidestep a concern with completeness for the sake of correcting an obvious injustice such as

---

[240] Sen (2009): 18-19, 231-235.
[241] Freeman (2010): 10.
[242] Moreover, Sen would also need to provide a theory regarding what these deontological considerations amount to.

"torture."[243] On Sen's account, despite our inability to make precise determinations as to how to weigh personal liberties against other concerns, we can nevertheless condemn torture and call for its elimination immediately.[244] Rawls's theory, on Sen's account, does not have this luxury—it *must* provide a solution to the weighing problem before it recommends a solution. That is, after all, the curse of transcendental theories of justice.

However, there are two problems with this reply. First of all, it is a mischaracterization of Rawls's position to assume that Rawls's theory of justice requires a *precise weighing* of the basic liberties against one another at the level of his two principles of justice. Instead, Rawls offers the general requirement that "liberty can be restricted only for the sake of liberty itself."[245] What this means is that we can only curtail a basic liberty if only to safeguard the "fully adequate scheme" of liberties that can be guaranteed for all.[246] However, at later stages—at the constitutional, legislative, and administrative (judges and citizens) stages—more precise applications can be sorted out which will require legal interpretation and information about the particular society we live in. Importantly, Rawls acknowledges that these stages are "often indeterminate:

---

[243] Sen (2006): 224: "We may acknowledge the possibility that liberties of different persons may, to some extent, conflict with each other (so that any fine-tuning of the demands of equal liberty may be hard to work out), and yet strongly agree that torturing accused people would be an unjust violation of liberty and that this injustice calls for an urgent rectification."

[244] Ibid., 223-224.

[245] TJ, 214.

[246] JF, 42.

it is not always clear which of several constitutions, or economic and social arrangements would be chosen."[247] Continuing, Rawls says that

> We must fall back upon a notion of quasi-pure procedural justice: laws and policies are just provided that they lie within the allowed range....This indeterminacy in the theory of justice is not in itself a defect. It is what we should expect. Justice as fairness will prove a worthwhile theory if it defines the range of justice more in accordance with our considered judgments than do existing theories, and if it singles out with greater sharpness the graver wrongs a society should avoid.[248]

Rawls's notion of "procedural justice" is important here, for it means that, *precisely how we weigh and apply the basic liberties in society will largely be procedural*. So long as our selection and application of policies abide by the priority of liberty rule, *whatever results from the good faith implementation of the principles of justice will itself be just*. What this means is the following: At the level of ideal theory, we cannot give a direct weight to the basic liberties other than they cannot be restricted except for the sake of other liberties and that the resulting set of liberties is always a fully adequate scheme for all. So long as this priority is followed and applied transparently to society, the resulting institutions, laws and policies will be just. We cannot expect any more from ideal theory than this.

If we bring this back to Sen's criticism, Rawls's indeterminacy is not as objectionable as Sen makes it out to be, for Sen does not see justice as procedural. Utilizing Rawls's method, we *can* expect to construct a justifiable position on the injustice of torture using the four-stage procedural sequence. Given the unlikelihood

---

[247] TJ, 176.
[248] TJ, 176.

that torture is necessary to preserve the other basic liberties, we can safely assume that it will be condemned at the end of the sequence. However, at no point in this deliberation must we decide, once and for all, what the precise weight the basic liberties must have in a consequentialist rank-ordering sense. Given the procedural understanding of the four-stage sequence, it is unlikely that such a precise weighing will be possible or expected from Rawls's theory. All justice as fairness aims to accomplish is to "single out with greater sharpness the graver wrongs a society should avoid."[249] Anything more than this sharper focus of the priority of liberty is outside the limits of ideal theory.

We can now turn to the second problem with Sen's criticism. Sen's approach is, in fact, more likely to lead to paralysis and indeterminacy in the negative sense than is Rawls's. Since Sen is a consequentialist, the problem of weighing considerations will be much more important for deciding what justice requires. For, suppose we have a conflict between torture and security. While Sen might argue that it is "obvious" that we condemn torture, it is difficult to see how it follows from his consequentialist reasoning without a clear account of how to weigh the deontological elements of his theory against one another. This will prevent his theory from providing a solution to the problem. In contrast, Rawls can assert that, so long as the reference to the priority of liberty is maintained and is publicly recognized to be a reasonable interpretation of it, the resulting outcome will be just. Hence, given Sen's complex account of

---

[249] TJ, 176.

consequentialism, his approach, by a twist of fortune, ends up being the more indeterminate when compared to Rawls's procedural approach.

(e) The Purpose of Ideal Theory

While the previous sections have attempted to defend Rawls's ideal theory from Sen's criticisms, it is important not to overstate our case. There is no reason to think that Rawls believes that his conception of justice is *all* we need when attempting to improve justice in society. We need to consult social and economic theory to aid us in implementing, for instance, the difference principle. Nor does he think that, without an ideal theory of justice, improvements in society are literally *impossible*. Instead, my argument is that it will be much more difficult and haphazard if we do not. As such, strictly speaking, an ideal theory of justice is neither necessary nor sufficient for advancing justice in society. However, this does not show that ideal theory is *pointless* or limited to a mere intellectual exercise. To see why, consider the following example: Suppose we want to perform surgery on a patient. It is strictly true that, using sterile gloves is neither necessary nor sufficient for a successful outcome. It is not necessary for it is quite possible to perform surgery on a patient without them, and it is not sufficient for you certainly require more than gloves to operate. But what does this philosophical analysis tell us about the *importance* of sterile gloves? Not much. Hence, there is a certain limitation in using necessary and sufficient conditions to determine the usefulness or value of an undertaking. By analogy, it is not clear what value there is to be had in using necessary and sufficient conditions to determine the legitimacy or illegitimacy of ideal theory.

There is, to be fair, a certain intuitive appeal to what Sen is highlighting as an apparent problem with our thinking about justice. After all, if we can readily identify serious problems of injustice—malnutrition, famine, lack of access to health and education—why do we still need an ideal theory of justice? Do we not have sufficient agreement upon the relevant values of fairness, rights, and well-being to devote our intellectual energy to provide solutions to these concrete problems?

I will make just two final remarks here. First, as rehearsed earlier, some persons regard the cases of injustice that Sen highlights as humanitarian failings or as unfortunate conditions that persons face in life. That is, they do not see them as uniquely problems of justice, but as other types of regrettable features of the world. As such, it is one responsibility of the philosopher to systemize our normative judgments so as to provide justification and coherence to our conviction that something is an instance of injustice. If this sounds like an idle proclamation from the ivory tower, one need only descend from it to find a cornucopia of different views and perspectives on what the appropriate response is to various failings in society. It is the hope, albeit a distant hope, that a theory of justice might be able to provide a vision that organizes and gives force to our demands of society and its citizens in the most complete manner possible. This is not to suggest that Sen has not done a great deal towards this goal. His work has been invaluable in addressing serious problems in nonideal theory and in the legislative stages of achieving justice.[250] Nevertheless, it is Rawls's view that a concept of justice that is based on the social contract tradition will ultimately resonate with us far more than a consequentialist vision will. I cannot, of course, provide a full argument in support of this here, but it is important to recognize that these visions do find their way, eventually, to the activists and reformers that change society from below.

My second remark to Sen's challenge is to perhaps present the role of ideal theory as similar to the work of mathematicians or theoretical physicists and to see the task of solving complex problems to be the result of a "division of labor" of sorts between various domains of inquiry. The thought is, just as the work of mathematicians[251] or physicists can seem "distant" to the task of constructing a bridge or building an airplane, it would be a mistake to deem them pointless, for they typically provide the impetus for further breakthroughs in development. In the same way, our ideal theories of justice aim to provide the clearest expression of our deepest help convictions about how reasonable and rational citizens can live and cooperate with one another. While this more abstract approach appears distant to the relief of widespread malnutrition and the subjection of women across the globe, it is the hope that Rawls's principles become further entrenched in our thinking and can be called upon with greater regularity and firmness when reform is necessary—either by emphasizing the importance of the worst-off members of society, or by highlighting the importance of

---

[250] For Sen's groundbreaking work on famines, see Sen, Amartya. *Poverty and Famines*. Oxford Clarendon Press, 1981. In addition, Sen has greatly reformed economics and utilitarianism to move beyond mere preference satisfaction or welfare as the appropriate metric of justice. See Sen, Amartya. *Commodities and Capabilities*. Oxford University Press, 1999.

[251] Though, as I shall argue in the final chapter, justice is nevertheless *practical* as opposed to theoretical.

equality of opportunity over concerns of increased GDP. This shift in our thinking can take generations to fully be comprehended, and so it is premature to reject Rawls's model as inert with respect to the demands for justice.

Chapter 5: Justice and Empirical Facts

I. Introduction

The central purpose of this chapter is to explore the relationship between principles of justice on the one hand, and empirical facts about human nature and society on the other. One reason to investigate this connection is because it is common to think that our normative principles should, in some way, be informed by facts about the world. We might say that, for instance, the fact that human beings are only capable of limited altruism should affect our choice of principles to govern behavior and our institutions. We might also think that facts about human psychology and human motivational capacities should set the limits for what normative principles can require from us. For instance, as we have already seen in earlier chapters, Rawls regularly appeals to facts about our moral psychology and the stability of society to question the merits of utilitarianism and to advocate for his own principles. Indeed, Rawls's commitment to a realistic utopia depends upon on this methodology, as it ensures that our normative principles are suitably grounded in the world and establishes that justice is fundamentally achievable for creatures such as ourselves.

However, the method of appealing to facts to argue for or against principles of justice has been left unchallenged thus far, despite its prima facie plausibility. As such, it is still an open question whether this methodology for thinking about justice is acceptable. And so, the question that confronts us is the following: *Should* our political principles be justified or constrained by empirical facts related to human beings and their social life? And, if so, which facts should be relevant, and in what way?

Numerous philosophers have weighed in on this debate in strikingly diverse ways. To illustrate, consider the following claims:

First, according to John Rawls:

> In justice as fairness the first principles of justice depend upon those general beliefs about human nature and how society works....First principles are not, in a constructivist view, independent of such beliefs, nor...true of all possible worlds. In particular, they depend on the rather specific features and limitations of human life that give rise to the circumstances of justice.[252]

In contrast, we have G.A. Cohen, who asserts the very opposite view:

> The thesis to be defended here contradicts...that our beliefs about principles should reflect facts about human nature, such as the fact that human beings are liable to pain, or the fact that they are capable of sympathy for each other, and also facts about human social organization, such as the tendency for people to encounter collective action problems, or for societies to be composed of individuals who have diverse interests and conflicting opinions.[253]

Continuing, Cohen claims:

> Facts are irrelevant in the determination of fundamental principles of justice. Facts of human nature and human society...make no difference to the very nature of justice itself.[254]

This foundational disagreement between Rawls and Cohen about the role of facts in our conception of justice will serve as the primary focus of this chapter. However, as the

---

[252] Rawls, John. "Kantian Constructivism in Moral Theory," in *Collected Papers*, ed. Samuel Freeman, Harvard University Press, 1999: 351. Quoted by Samuel Freeman in "Constructivism, Facts and Moral Justification," in *Contemporary Debates in Political Philosophy*, eds. Thomas Christiano and John Christman, Blackwell Publishing, 2009: 41.

[253] Cohen, G.A. *Rescuing Justice and Equality.* Harvard University Press, 2008: 231.

[254] Ibid., 285.

questions before us are quite broad, we would do best to specify more clearly the kinds of issues that are at stake in this disagreement.

In the first section, I consider the question of whether Rawls's two principles of justice are truly the *fundamental* principles of justice given their reliance on facts, or if, as Cohen charges, they are instead "rules of regulation" that depend upon a more ultimate principle that is "fact-free."[255] I argue that Cohen misunderstands what fundamental principles of justice are and that his charge that all fundamental principles must be independent of facts is incorrect.

In the second section, I discuss a set of facts—limited beneficence and moderate scarcity—called the "circumstances of justice," which are said to be the preconditions for the emergence of justice itself.[256] Cohen and others have challenged this view, arguing that justice does not depend upon factual circumstances at all and that justice applies everywhere. In response, I defend Rawls (and Hume) who assert the importance of these facts for determining when justice arises.

In the third section, I provide a general account of what kinds of facts are permitted in the original position when deliberating about principles of justice. I argue that the selection of facts that are relevant are based on several criteria: stability, publicity, generating *fair* terms of agreement, and even making agreement possible. The facts that are included will be general facts about human nature, our higher order interests, human psychology, and our empirical understanding of the world and social

[255] Ibid., 19.
[256] JF, 84.

life. In addition, I discuss the importance of the veil of ignorance in determining which facts are *irrelevant* for justice. I argue that our conception of ourselves as free and equal requires us to hide certain facts from ourselves and our society to determine what justice requires.

Next, I turn to several criticisms of this account of the importance of facts by G.A. Cohen and David Estlund. Cohen rejects the relevance of facts, arguing that we have a concept of justice that is independent of them, and that concerns for notions such as stability are "absurd."[257] I reply on behalf of Rawls and emphasize that justice must be, at its core, practical for us and that stability must be directly relevant. David Estlund argues that facts about human nature that are permitted in the original position are objectionable on the grounds that not all features of human nature are morally acceptable and that we should be able to condemn them when they interfere with the demands of justice. I argue that the objectionable elements of human nature are not likely to occur in the well-ordered society, and that they are properly regarded as contingent features of ourselves, or "special psychologies." As such, they would not pose problems for stability.

II. Are Fundamental Principles of Justice "Fact-Free?"

Rawls believes that his two principles of justice—the guarantee of the equal basic liberties and the difference principle—are fundamental principles of justice.[258]

---

[257] Cohen (2008): 327.

[258] Rawls himself does not explicitly use the term "fundamental" to describe his principles in any of his texts. When I apply that term for Rawls, I am merely conveying the underlying idea that they are the most important regulating principle for justice. The term "fundamental" has been imposed on him by G.A.

They are regarded as having the highest authority and providing the final answer as to how we should arrange the basic structure of society, which includes the major legal, political, and economic institutions of society.[259] Rawls's principles are the consequence of a constructed decision procedure, called the original position, which organizes and systemizes our considered convictions about justice into one "coherent view."[260] Within the original position, we are allowed access to a set of facts about human psychology and human nature, as well as general facts about the natural and social sciences to aid us in our selection of principles. After utilizing this procedure to combine our considered convictions and our assessment of facts, we are then able to clearly arrive at and agree upon the most reasonable principles of justice for us--Rawls's two ordered principles—to regulate the conduct of institutions.

According to a series of criticisms by G.A. Cohen, however, Rawls has not actually described fundamental principles of justice at all. Because of his reliance on the original position and his appeal to a great number of facts inside the procedure, he has only found "rules of regulation" or *applied* principles of justice.[261] A truly fundamental principle of justice, for Cohen, cannot rely on any other facts or procedures. The reason for this is because, once we understand the justification for *why* these procedures and facts are relevant, we will be able to discover other more basic principles in our

---

Cohen and I will employ the term for the purposes of this dialectic with him. My own view is that we should regard Rawls's two principles of justice as the most *reasonable* principles of justice. I believe Rawls deliberately avoided the term "fundamental" as it would indicate that he believed his principles were "foundationalist" or "self-evident," neither of which is true.

[259] TJ, 6-7.

[260] TJ, 19.

[261] Cohen (2008): 253.

normative architecture. It is these principles which are genuinely fundamental principles of justice, not Rawls's two principles of justice.

Let us provide an example to illustrate Cohen's thesis and outline his basic method. For instance, let us examine the following common-sense normative principle: "One ought to arrive on-time to one's appointments." We might then wonder, is this principle a fundamental principle? Cohen's basic test for this is to ask what our justification for it is. Suppose I answered with the following reply: "If we arrive late to our appointments, other people will be inconvenienced and their plans will be disrupted."[262] Notice that my justification invoked a *fact*—the fact that people will be inconvenienced or that their plans would be disrupted. Why is this important? Because, whenever our justification for a principle requires a fact to support it, there must always be a *further* principle that explains why the fact is relevant. To put it in Cohen's language:

> Whenever a fact *F* confers support on a principle *P*, there is an explanation *why F* supports *P*, an explanation of how, that is, *F* represents a reason to endorse *P*.[263]

If Cohen is right, then we should be able to discover another more basic principle that explains why the fact of inconvenience is important. What might this principle be? Naturally, the following: "One ought not disrupt the plans of others or cause them inconveniences." And so, the complete argument and each of its premises would look like this:

---

[262] This is not the *only* possible justification, but it will serve to illustrate Cohen's thesis well.
[263] Ibid., 236.

(1) One ought not disrupt the plans of others or cause them inconveniences.
(2) If we arrive late to our appointments, other people will be inconvenienced and their plans will be disrupted.

Therefore,

(3) One ought to arrive on-time to one's appointments.

With the argument presented in this way, we can more clearly see that our original principle is really the *conclusion* to an argument that requires support from a fact and a more fundamental principle. And so, our original principle cannot be a fundamental principle.

But now we may then ask, is our new principle a fundamental principle, or is it justified by yet *another* fact and a further principle that explains the relevance of that fact? Let us examine our justification for why we ought not disrupt the plans of others or cause them inconveniences. Suppose I say: "Disrupting plans and inconveniencing others causes harm to people."[264] Notice again that my justification invokes a fact—that disrupting plans harms people. Using Cohen's method, we should be able to invoke a prior principle that explains why harm is relevant to the disruption of plans. This further principle might be, for instance, "one ought not harm others." With this, we can complete our original argument in the same manner as above. And so on, and so forth.

We can continue this process only for so long, however.[265] Eventually, Cohen believes that we will reach a point at which we can no longer appeal to facts to justify our principles. For Cohen, these points lie at the "summit of our convictions" and

[264] Again, we may disagree with this justification. We might argue that it involves the violation of promises, etc.

[265] "It is just implausible that a credible interrogation of that form might go on indefinitely: if you disagree, try to construct one, one that goes beyond citation of, say, five principles," Cohen (2008): 237.

represent genuine *fundamental principles.*[266] Moreover, these principles must always be *fact-free*, for if ever we invoked a fact for their justification, it would always entail the existence of a further principle to explain that fact's relevance. Cohen states his conclusion as follows:

> A principle can respond to (that is, be grounded in) a fact only because it is also a response to a more ultimate principle that is not a response to a fact: accordingly, if principles respond to facts, then *the principles at the summit of our conviction are grounded in no facts whatsoever.*[267]

Whether or not we believe that the principle "do not harm others" is truly the final resting point of our convictions is, of course, up for further investigation which I have not tried to recreate here. Nevertheless, the important lesson is that Cohen's toolkit can be applied to any principle that we proffer as a fundamental principle, including principles of justice. If, in our justification for it, we state a fact, then we can reiterate Cohen's methodology any number of times until we reach the pinnacle of our beliefs—the top of which will necessarily contain a fact-free fundamental principle. And so, according to Cohen, "every-fact sensitive principle reflects a fact-insensitive principle."[268]

With this argumentative strategy at hand, Cohen then argues that Rawls's two principles of justice cannot possibly be the fundamental principles of justice, for Rawls justifies these principles by invoking a plethora of facts to do so. For instance, let us examine some of the arguments that Rawls marshals for the difference principle (DP),

---

[266] Ibid., 291.
[267] Ibid., 229, emphasis added.
[268] Ibid., 237.

according to which inequalities are permitted only if they benefit the least advantaged members of society.[269]

First, we might justify the *DP* based on a notion of reciprocity.[270] The underlying idea would be that persons would not accept a principle, such as the principle of utility, in which inequalities might be allowed that required the worst-off members to sacrifice their interests for the sake of the majority. Such a principle would go against the fair terms of social cooperation in which citizens work together to produce the goods and services of society on terms that are acceptable to all fully cooperative members. The difference principle, in contrast, expresses a commitment to reciprocal relations between persons by guaranteeing that any inequalities are for the sake of those who are least well-off and that their interests are never merely sacrificed for the greater good of others. As Freeman notes:

> The main argument in favor of the difference principle depends on a strong idea of *reciprocity* (JF §36). In a society structured by the difference principle gains to those more advantaged are never made at the expense of those less advantaged; instead, any gains to the more advantaged always benefit also the least advantaged, and do so more than any other alternative measure.[271]

Second, we may also justify the difference principle as necessary to preserve a sense of self-respect among persons, which, according to Rawls, is "the most important

---

[269] TJ, 54.
[270] JF, 133: "[The difference principle] has many desirable features and formulates in a simple way an idea of reciprocity."
[271] Freeman, Samuel. "The Original Position," *The Stanford Encyclopedia of Philosophy*. https://plato.stanford.edu/entries/original-position/#ArgForDifPri [2014, September 9th].

primary good."[272] Self-respect is "a psychological attitude that includes a sense that our individual lives matter and are worth living."[273] In a society governed by a principle that permits the worst-off members to sacrifice the goods and opportunities necessary to pursue a rational life plan, their sense of self-respect in society would be damaged for they would not view their contributions as worthwhile or valuable. The implicit message in society for these members would be that they are expendable and that the fruits of their labor are not important for society. It is difficult for citizens subject to these outcomes to view their lives as being socially valued.[274]

Returning to Cohen's argument, we can use his methodology to examine the justification of Rawls's commitment to the difference principle.[275] Since the difference principle relies upon facts about reciprocity and psychological attitudes about self-respect, we would be compelled to make the following argument:

(1) The difference principle best promotes self-respect between persons and establishes a relationship of reciprocity.
(2) We ought to promote self-respect and encourage relationships based on reciprocity.

Therefore,

(3) We ought to endorse the *DP*.

With the argument spelled out in this form, Cohen would argue that premise (2) is the more fundamental principle of justice, namely, the principle that "we ought to promote

---

[272] TJ, 386.

[273] Freeman (2009): 46.

[274] Hence, Rawls highlights how self-respect has a social basis: "Self-respect depends upon and is encouraged by certain public features of basic social institutions, how they work and how people who accept these arrangements are expected to (and normally do) regard and treat one another," PL, 319.

[275] There are, of course other justifications for the difference principle, such as the importance of maximin, but I am using the concern for reciprocity and self-respect as examples to illustrate Cohen's thesis.

self-respect and encourage relationships based on reciprocity." This would serve to show that the *DP* is not, in fact, the fundamental principle of justice.

Now, we can investigate this principle further if we think that we must appeal to another fact to affirm it. We might think the following fact is necessary for its justification: "By promoting self-respect and reciprocal relationships between persons, we express a commitment to their freedom and equality."[276] And, as such, the fact-free principle that justifies this fact would be the following: "respect the freedom and equality of persons." The summit of our convictions has thus been reached.[277]

Does Cohen's strategy succeed? Must Rawls affirm the fact-free principle "respect the freedom and equality of persons" as the *fundamental principle of justice*? Are Rawls's two principles of justice merely applied principles of these more fundamental types given their reliance on facts?

There are at least two ways to respond to this conclusion. First, I will challenge the notion that a fundamental principle of justice must be identical with the summit of our normative convictions. Second, I will argue that our most basic normative convictions stand in need of interpretation and cannot stand alone as principles of justice.

---

[276] There are other elements related to the importance of self-respect, such as a discussion of the importance of stability. However, for the purposes of this section, I have chosen the commitment to freedom and equality as one possibility.

[277] Cohen's own belief about what would be the summit for Rawls's justification of the *DP* would be the following thoughts: "One ought not to cause too much inequality," and "promote the condition of the worst off," Cohen (2008): 259, 261. But this cannot be true for Rawls, for the reason why too much inequality is problematic is because of the potential loss of self-respect that may result in citizens. See TJ, 468. Similarly, we promote the condition of the worst-off members not because of a detached concern for the poor, but because it would unreasonable to ask the worst-off members to sacrifice gains for themselves for the greater gains of others. This would violate our respect for them.

(a) Fundamental Principles are Domain Specific

To begin, I will attempt to show that our most basic normative convictions do not necessarily equate to a fundamental principle within the same domain of inquiry.

Let me illustrate with an example from the empirical sciences to demonstrate this thesis. Suppose I state Newton's third law of motion as a *fundamental principle of classical mechanics*. The third law is as follows:

> When one body exerts a force on a second body, the second body simultaneously exerts a force equal in magnitude and opposite in direction on the first body.[278]

Now, using Cohen's methodology, suppose I demand a justification for the law. We will presumably need to appeal to another *fact* to do so, such as the following:

> F1: Our observations and measurements of the world corroborate Newton's Third Law of Motion.

And, continuing, implicit in this justification is the further fact:

> F2: Our empirical observations represent the reality of the world.

We can certainly continue this line of inquiry for several more steps, but suppose that we have reached the summit of our convictions after probing the justification of our physical laws in this manner.[279] The important point here is to notice what *type* of claim we have arrived at. This certainly does not look like a *fundamental principle of motion*, or of physics. After all, what would it mean to say that "our empirical

---

[278] Wikipedia contributors. "Newton's Laws of Motion." *Wikipedia, The Free Encyclopedia.* Web. 12 April 2017 <https://en.wikipedia.org/wiki/Newton%27s_laws_of_motion>.

[279] Further steps will inevitably involve claims about induction, or, in the case of Hume, a claim about the relevance of custom. Nevertheless, it is not necessary to resolve the problem of induction for the purposes of my argument here, which is simply to demonstrate that, *wherever we end up*, the principle will be nothing like a fundamental principle of physics.

observations represent the reality of the world" is a fundamental principle of physics? Instead, it looks like a *principle of justification* that we must implicitly endorse in our commitments to fundamental physical laws.

In other words, just because we have a principle—like a fundamental principle of physics—that requires further principles to establish it, such as an epistemological or justificatory principle, it does not mean that the status of those principles is no longer fundamental.

If this is true, then what would it mean for something to be classified as a fundamental principle, then? Put simply, it must be the most basic principle *within a particular domain* of inquiry. For physics, a fundamental principle should be the ultimate principle or principles that describe the interactions of matter. The claim that "our empirical observations represent the reality of the world" offers no such description, and so is not a fundamental principle of physics, even though it is needed to justify those principles.

Let us apply this conclusion to Cohen's criticism of Rawls. By parity of reasoning, we should be able to defend Rawls by arguing that the "difference principle" and the commitment to "respect the freedom and equality of persons" are not the same type of principle. Even though the latter is required in our justification for the former, it does not follow that "respect the freedom and equality of persons" is a fundamental principle of *justice*.

According to Rawls, justice is about what principles we should adopt to regulate our institutions that determine the distribution of resources and the assignment of rights and liberties given that persons see themselves as free and equal and understand society as a fair system of social cooperation.[280] The principle "respect the freedom and equality of persons" is not a principle that, on its own, can settle the central problem of justice. The freedom and equality of persons is instead a normative conception that we *start with* and must then be interpreted and reflected in our principles of justice and the selection procedure for determining them.

Rawls's two principles of justice, by contrast, *do* address the central problem of justice, and should be interpreted as the most basic and fundamental principles we can appeal to in that domain.[281] As such, these different principles operate at separate levels and should therefore not be compared against one another as suitable candidates for a fundamental principle of justice.[282]

One objection we might make here is that "respect the freedom and equality of persons" *is* within the same domain as the difference principle—after all, they are both *normative*. However, one consequence of this reply is that we must then deny that justice is a separate domain of inquiry from the domain of the normative in general.

---

[280] JF, 7-8.

[281] Freeman (2009) notes: "What makes a substantive principle of conduct fundamental is not that it is self-evident or otherwise without normative justification, but that it is the ultimate standard for determining conduct and there are no more basic principles of which it is an application," p. 44.

[282] For a related discussion of this distinction, see Freeman (2009): 42-46.

Rawls certainly believes that justice involves a distinct form of practical reasoning, one that is not simply the result of direct deductive reasoning from basic moral principles.[283]

Let me illustrate this disagreement with another analogy with the sciences. We might think that physics and biology, despite being in the same category of the "empirical," may still be separate domains of inquiry and subject to different principles. That is, just as there are fundamental principles of biology, there are also distinct fundamental principles of physics, even if we admit that biological principles *depend upon* principles of physics. Of course, this is controversial and involves debates within the philosophy of science about the problem of reductionism and the ontological status of laws of nature.[284] Nevertheless, insofar as we are inclined to see the independence of the political from the moral, or the independence of the different subjects of the sciences, we should not accept Cohen's demonstration as a successful refutation of Rawls's fundamental principles of justice.

(b) Our Basic Normative Convictions Must be Interpreted

I now wish to examine the second reply to Cohen's argument which involves Rawls's own stated understanding of how the justification for his principles of justice is

---

[283] Cohen's methodology may perhaps unearth the fundamental principle of justice within a consequentialist moral framework more perspicuously, but Rawls would reject that understanding of justice. I will defend this in the next section.

[284] For a general discussion of these problems see McShea, Daniel and Alex Rosenberg. *Philosophy of Biology*. Routledge, 2008: 32-64. For a discussion of how all scientific disciplines face the same problems of finding truly generalizable laws see Cartwright, Nancy. *How the Laws of Physics Lie*. Oxford University Press, 1983. And for a defense of the reality of biology "laws" in the form of stable generalizations see Godfrey-Smith, Peter. *Philosophy of Biology*. Princeton University Press, 2014: 11-28. If we dislike the example with biology, we may perhaps use chemistry instead.

supposed to work. Let me begin with two quotes from Rawls near the final pages of *A Theory of Justice*.[285] Rawls says:

> The principles of justice are not derived from the notion of respect for persons....it is precisely these ideas that call for interpretation.[286]

Rawls continues:

> Once the conception of justice is at hand, however, the ideas of respect and human dignity can be given a more definite meaning. Among other things, respect for persons is shown by treating them in ways that they can see to be justified....The theory of justice provides a rendering of these ideas *but we cannot start out from them*. There is no way to avoid the complications of the original position, or of similar construction, if our notions of respect and the natural basis of equality are to be systematically presented.[287]

There are several points that are important in these passages. First, Rawls does not view the principles of justice as being "derived" from notions of respect or equality.[288] Instead, Rawls requires that these concepts be "interpreted" and represented in some way. Otherwise, we are left without a clear meaning of these concepts and little can be deduced from them on their own. To illustrate, many conceptions of justice—utilitarian, libertarian, egalitarian—assert the importance of respecting the freedom and equality of persons as foundational for their normative frameworks. However, it would be somewhat bizarre to claim that all utilitarians, libertarians and egalitarians therefore *agree on the fundamental principles of justice* simply because they all recognize their endorsement of the fact-free normative

---

[285] I thank James Gledhill for pointing these quotes out to me at the Pacific APA in 2012.
[286] TJ, 513.
[287] TJ, 513, emphasis added.
[288] We should expect that the same would hold for freedom as well.

commitment to respect the freedom and equality of persons. After all, if everyone already agrees, then what is everyone debating about, exactly?[289]

Instead, we should investigate how each conception of justice interprets these more basic normative judgments and represents them. For instance, many utilitarians represent the commitment to equality by imagining an impartial spectator as encompassing everyone's desires and acting upon them as one unified legislator.[290] This procedure reflects the commitment that each person's desires should be counted for equally. Hobbes, on the other hand, represents the freedom and equality of persons by describing each person as equally capable of destroying one another in a state of nature in which there are no laws or rules in place to constrain behavior. Rawls, in contrast, reflects these concepts through the veil of ignorance in the original position. The *OP* represents the freedom of persons by assuming that all persons have an interest in developing their capacity to pursue and, upon reflection, refine their conception of the good. It expresses their equality by having each person represented in the choice situation "symmetrically," by concealing morally arbitrary factors about themselves, in addition to assuming that each person has an equal voice in the formulation of a public conception of justice that each person can endorse.[291]

---

[289] Cohen's answer here is that everyone is debating about how to *apply* principles of justice to the world. But would we say that physicists agree on the fundamental principles of physics and merely disagree about how to *apply* the principle, "our empirical observations mirror the world?" Perhaps, but it is difficult to see what is gained by this argumentative strategy.

[290] Smith, Adam. *The Theory of Moral Sentiments,* ed. by D.D. Raphael and A.L. Macfie. Oxford University Press, 1976.

[291] JF, 18.

Given these diverse ways in which freedom and equality are represented in different methodological devices, we can see how each perspective highlights different fundamental features of persons: Hobbes believes the core of who we are is best represented by our self-interested behavior in the absence of a sovereign authority; utilitarians believe that the person is fundamentally defined by their desires whatever they turn out to be; and Rawls believes that we are persons endowed with "two fundamental powers" to (1) pursue a rational plan of life and (2) develop and act upon a sense of justice in which we recognize our responsibility for our own ends and endorse the necessity to govern our socially cooperative activity on terms that are reasonable to all.[292]

This is, of course, not the place for a full argument about the merits of these different approaches. Our main task here is to demonstrate how the commitment to the freedom and equality of persons, on its own, cannot settle the question of justice by means of a kind of "derivation," as Rawls says. These ideas must be interpreted and represented into the most appropriate model and tested against numerous other considered convictions that we have. How we select which decision procedure to use—the original position or the impartial spectator—will rely upon these other judgments that we have, including input from other facts about our moral architecture. It does not make sense to regard any of these elements as the most fundamental aspect of justice, for they all operate at various levels of our judgment. Rawls believes that it is the

---

[292] PL, 19.

conclusion to this "reflective equilibrium" between all the elements that determines what the principles of justice ultimately will be.[293]

In reply, Cohen rejects Rawls's holistic approach to justice,[294] and he believes that, despite Rawls's insistence on the importance of reflective equilibrium, if we probe his architectonic theory deeply enough, a fundamental principle will emerge that ultimately informs us how to justify all the parts. To illustrate, Cohen first presses us to articulate the basis upon which we select the original position. He states:

> We have to reckon not only with the principles justified by the original position procedure, but also with *the principles that justify that procedure*. Procedure is not ultimate: as Rawls says, not everything is constructed. And the reason why the constructive procedure is judged appropriate is, to put the matter simply, that it reflects the 'conception' of persons as free and equal. But that way of conceiving them either embodies or presupposes a fact-insensitive principle.[295]

It is clear that Cohen acknowledges that a conception of free and equal persons will serve as the baseline in our determination of the original position. Indeed, he argues that it "embodies" and "presupposes" this "fact-insensitive principle." So far so good. We have already addressed this concern. However, he then argues that "it is not obvious" what *justifies* the conception of free and equal persons and how this conception yields our judgements about the original position, and ultimately our principles of justice.[296] Presumably, Cohen believes that there may be yet another fact-

---

[293] TJ, 18-19.
[294] Cohen (2008): 241-243.
[295] Ibid., 241, emphasis added.
[296] Ibid., 241.

free principle that answers these questions, and that, once unearthed, we will be able to fully justify Rawls's methodology.

In order to buttress the reply to Cohen's challenge that I have already provided above, I will attempt to show, in two parts, that Cohen's pressings will not yield fruitful results, and that fundamental principles of justice are not of the foundationalist nature that Cohen asserts them to be. First, I will attempt to briefly unearth the importance of our conception of ourselves as free and equal according to Rawls's "Kantian Interpretation" in his *Theory of Justice*.[297] Second, I will turn to Rawls's more limited approach to the conception of the person that is political in nature, as developed in *Political Liberalism*.[298] Whichever approach we use, the fundamental principle that lies at Cohen's "summit" will not be a fundamental principle of justice.

(c) The Kantian Argument

According to Rawls, the selection of the original position is "based upon Kant's notion of autonomy,"[299] and that "a person is acting autonomously when the principles of his action are chosen by him as the most adequate possible expression of his nature as a free and equal rational being."[300] When we enter the original position, the veil of ignorance hides the *contingent* features of ourselves, such as our particular ends or desires, so that when we rationally choose principles, we are not acting heteronomously.

---

[297] See TJ, 221-227. Also see Rawls, John. "Kantian Constructivism in Moral Theory," *The Journal of Philosophy* 77, no. 9, (1980): 515-572.
[298] PL, 29-34.
[299] TJ, 221.
[300] TJ, 222.

That is, we are not selecting principles based on our contingent ends.[301] Instead, we are selecting principles based upon our fundamental capacity to pursue a rational plan of life, *whatever it happens to be*.[302] As such, in the original position, we are all **equals**, blinded by our particular ends, and we are acting **freely**, as we are not bound by them in our selection of principles.[303]

Finally, in addition to having the fundamental capacity to pursue a rational plan of life, we have the desire to act upon a sense of justice. For Rawls, this desire "derives from the desire to express most fully what we are or can be, namely free and equal rational beings with a liberty to choose."[304] In this sense, our sense of justice is based upon our desire to express who we fundamentally are when we select and employ our principles of justice. We do not want our principles to reflect who we might contingently be, constrained by our particular aims or desires.[305] We aim for principles that express our fundamental nature.[306]

We may then present the entire argument as follows:

---

[301] Rawls says: "The principles he acts upon are not adopted because of...the specific things that he happens to want, " TJ, 222.

[302] This is how Rawls derives the concern for the primary goods—as they are the goods that anyone would rationally want, whichever final ends we select for ourselves. TJ, 223.

[303] Rawls says: "Thus men exhibit their freedom, their independence from the contingencies of nature and society, by acting in ways they would acknowledge in the original position," TJ, 225.

[304] TJ, 225.

[305] When we act unjustly, Rawls says: "We have acted as though we belonged to a lower order, as though we were a creature whose first principles are decided by natural contingencies," TJ, 225.

[306] We can contrast this approach with the utilitarian conception of the person which decides principles of justice, at its core, *heteronomously*. Even though the impartial spectator represents a kind of equality between persons, it does not represent their freedom, for the persons are selecting principles based upon *everyone's particular aims or desires*. For Rawls, the move from a single person's desires to *all* persons' desires does not solve the problem. It then just describes a "kingdom of ends" that is heteronomous.

(1) We are fundamentally autonomous beings who are free and equal.
(2) We desire to select principles of justice that represent our essential aims, not our contingent ones.
(3) The Original Position utilizes the veil of ignorance to represent everyone equally and allows us to select principles in accordance with our freedom.

Therefore,

(4) The Original Position is the best methodological device for determining principles of justice.
(5) The Difference Principle is the only principle that persons would agree to in the Original Position to regulate the distribution of resources.[307]

Therefore,

(6) The Difference Principle is a fundamental principle of justice.

This is, of course, a long and complex argument, with still yet more premises to be filled in.[308] Nevertheless, the important stages of the argument have been filled in for our purposes of answering Cohen's objection.

Returning to Cohen and his fact-finding mission, what would the fundamental, fact-free principle of justice be in this long chain of argument? I believe Cohen must claim that the fundamental principle required to justify the entire string of premises would be as follows:

---

[307] This argument requires arguments that we have already outlined earlier about the importance of reciprocity and self-respect.

[308] There are still the "circumstances of justice" and other facts about human nature and society that are needed to determine what the primary goods will be. I will address the circumstances of justice and claims about human nature later. In addition, because of Rawls's commitment to "holism," it will generally be very difficult to list all the reasons and considerations that go into the justification for his principles of justice. I have aimed only to focus on the most central aspects for the purposes of Cohen's argument, leaving other elements to be filled in. This should also serve to demonstrate why Rawls does not generally regard his principles of justice to be based strictly on a deductive proof. Instead, Rawls thinks we can at most provide "the balance of reasons" in favor of a particular conception, JF, 133-134. However, Rawls does aim to be able to "present the parties' reasoning" as "fully deductive, a kind of moral geometry," though he admits nevertheless that "our reasoning is highly intuitive and falls far short of that ideal," JF, 133.

P: We ought to represent ourselves as we essentially are and select principles of justice that reflect our fundamental nature.

Why is this the fundamental fact-free principle? Because when we ask what justifies the claim that we ought to select principles based upon our autonomy, we must reply with the claim that we "desire to express most fully what we are."[309] And so, we arrive at the pinnacle of our normative judgements to represent ourselves as who we fundamentally are.[310]

It should be apparent that, from the previous arguments outlined before, the same kinds of objections will be relevant here, so Cohen's instance that we probe the depths of our normative judgments will still yield principles that stand in need of interpretation. For in what sense is the principle "we must represent ourselves as we essentially are" a fundamental principle of justice? Does it adequately serve as a public criterion with which to organize our institutions? Can it be appealed to as having final authority in the distribution of resources? Or is it simply too vague and indeterminate on its own? These considerations should give us pause with respect to whether our most basic normative convictions are identical with fundamental principles of justice.

---

[309] TJ, 225. Rawls says: "The parties...have a desire to express their nature as rational and equal members...with precisely this liberty to choose."

[310] Of course, we may object that this makes Rawls's entire project heteronomous after all, as it is based on a desire. But this desire is really the sense of justice. Without it, we could not be the kinds of rational and moral beings that we are. To be clear, these arguments are notoriously complex, and relate to whether Kant's own demonstration of why freedom is valuable can be made without an appeal to human desires. For a discussion of these problems see Guyer, Paul. *Kant.* Routledge, 2006. For a different criticism of Rawls's Kantian interpretation as being heteronomous, see Johnson, Oliver. "The Kantian Interpretation," *Ethics* vol. 85, no. 1 (1974): 58-66. The central argument here is that Rawls's veil of ignorance does not accurately reflect the freedom of persons because they are still selecting principles based on desires and wants—namely, the desire to attain primary goods and pursue a conception of the good.

It may be objected here that Kant was surely able to derive fundamental normative principles from the autonomy of human beings. After all, the categorical imperative is supposed to be the supreme principle of morality and is implicit in our fundamental nature as free and rational creatures. From it, we are able to derive both our moral duties and the doctrine of Right. However, Rawls parts ways with Kant in this regard:

> The freedom of pure intelligences...are outside the range of the theory. Kant may have meant his doctrine to apply to all rational beings as such and therefore that men's social situation in the world is to have no role in determining the first principles of justice. If so, this is another difference between justice as fairness and Kant's theory.[311]

Rawls, instead, attempts to "recast" Kant's theory "within the scope of an empirical theory."[312] This is perhaps because Rawls must have rejected Kant's account of justice as being simply an application of the categorical imperative to the empirical world. Or, he may not have believed that *synthetic a priori* judgments were possible, or that Kant could not sufficiently demonstrate that the value of freedom was not based on human desire. Whatever his reasons, if Rawls rejected these elements, then it would make sense that he believed that the fundamental nature of justice would *have* to be empirical. There would be no other way to proceed. And if this is true, then Cohen's

---

[311] TJ, 226.
[312] TJ, 227.

strategy to unearth fact-free principles will eventually lead to a dead end that will require the input from facts to allow us to proceed any further.[313]

(d) The Argument from Political Liberalism

I mentioned that there were two forks we might take in addressing Cohen's challenge—to either explore the full Kantian strategy, or to reject it and aim for a more modest approach based on the arguments from *Political Liberalism*. Let us examine that second fork now.

There are numerous problems with the more ambitious approach to justify Rawls's conception of justice in an ideal of autonomy and practical agency,[314] the most important of which that it was not sustainable to premise the conception of the person on a comprehensive doctrine.[315] Rawls believed that there would not be legitimate grounds for agreement in an overlapping consensus if his conception of justice required the adoption of a singular account of practical agency as part of the fundamental nature of persons. Rawls realized this, and, as Paul Guyer points out: "Rawls may have been wise to eschew any attempt to demonstrate that actual human beings *must* adopt the conception of themselves from which his constructivist justification of the principles of

---

[313] Cohen may argue that it is good to know where our dead-ends are (which is really another name for the summit of our judgments), but these won't be fundamental principles of justice; they will be the starting points from which to build a theory of justice.

[314] However, for a contemporary attempt to rescue Kant (and Rawls) from these difficulties, see Korsgaard, Christine. *Self-Constitution*. Oxford University Press, 2009.

[315] Rawls says: "Kant's doctrine is a comprehensive moral view in which the ideal of autonomy has a regulative role for all of life. This makes it incompatible with the political liberalism of justice as fairness." PL, 99.

justice begins."[316] Instead, Rawls addresses his conception of justice only to people who *already conceive themselves in this way*. Guyer continues: "Rawls's entire argument for the principles of justice is *analytical*, beginning with a concept that may or may not be accepted by any actual human being or beings,"[317] and is "aimed only at making clear to such people what principles of justice they need to adopt in order to be able to live a social life that conforms to the conception of a person that each person in a group of such people wishes be realized for all."[318]

In other words, Rawls's constructivism is limited to the arguments that *follow from* a conception of the person. The conception of the person is simply taken as given—which for Rawls means in *Political Liberalism*, contained within the liberal democratic political culture.[319] As such, it is true that, insofar as people reject this conception of the person, they will not be inclined to see Rawls's methodology as particularly gripping or applicable to them. This does not mean, of course, that we cannot provide arguments in its favor, or "present it in a very attractive light."[320] Rather, it merely means that it "cannot be derived from any non-controvertible premise that any human being must accept."[321]

---

[316] Guyer, Paul. "Constructivism and Self-Constitution," in *Kant on Practical Justification: Interpretive Essays*, ed. by Mark Timmons and Sorin Baiasu. Oxford University Press, 2013: 178-179.
[317] Ibid., 178.
[318] Ibid., 176.
[319] "The basis of this view lie in fundamental ideas of the public political culture," PL, 97.
[320] Guyer (2013): 180.
[321] Ibid., 180. This will provide even more problems for Cohen, as it means that the attempt to derive principles from non-controvertible or self-evident premises will not be possible.

For Rawls, the reasons that we usher in its favor will be based on a variety of implicit considered convictions and judgements that citizens make in liberal democratic societies about the centrality of their conception of the good, their capacity to act upon a sense of justice, and their conception of society as based on fair terms of cooperation.[322] In addition, there will be the recognition of reasonable pluralism and the burdens of judgment that characterize democratic life, coupled with the realization that one cannot live in a political society unified by a single conception of the good without unacceptable state coercion.[323] Importantly, these considerations do not rely upon a particular conception of the good, and can be endorsed in an overlapping consensus among members within society.[324] When we put all the arguments and considerations together, we should arrive at a political conception of the person, which should be seen as the most feasible way to provide coherence to our judgements as citizens in liberal democratic societies.

What implications does this more modest method of justification have for Cohen's strategy against Rawls? Framed in this way, the fact-free fundamental principle of justice would then have to be a complex multitude of considerations all taken together that mutually reinforce each other. Perhaps something of the following:

> **P2: We ought to conceive of ourselves in the most reasonable way—as one that provides coherence to our judgements within a liberal democratic society and as one that can serve as the basis for an overlapping consensus.**

---

[322] PL, 93.
[323] Rawls says: "The burdens of judgement set limits on what can be reasonably justified to others...It is unreasonable for us to use political power to repress comprehensive views." PL, 61.
[324] PL, 101.

To test whether this is truly fundamental, we may again ask if there are any facts that are required to affirm it. However, as we test the different elements—the limitation on liberal democratic societies, the concern for coherence, or the desire for an overlapping consensus—we will find that there will be an interconnecting web of considerations, none of which is alone at the pinnacle of our convictions. Instead, we will uncover the importance of *justification to others* and securing the basis for rational and reasonable *agreement*; or, on my own view, a view of justice as *realistically utopian*.[325]

However, these are distinct considered convictions that we have, and it would be a mischaracterization of them to consider them fundamental principles of justice. We can return to an illustration with the sciences to conclude this section. If we ask, "What is the aim of physics?," we are not asking for the fundamental principles of physics, such as the Principles of String Theory or Einstein's Principles of Relativity. We would answer that physics is about discovering the laws that underlie physical reality. We may also ask, "What are the methodological constraints on physics?" We may answer that we should utilize the scientific method to devise principles that are capable of being tested through observation. And finally, we may ask, "What are some virtues of fundamental principles of physics?" And we could say that principles ought to be subject to Ockham's Razor and should be parsimonious and simplistic. As we can see, none of

---

[325] At some level, however, Rawls will not see the importance of finding a single conviction that justifies all the others downstream, for Rawls does not see foundationalism as the appropriate method of normative theorizing and instead relies on reflective equilibrium and a coherentism about justification. See JF, 29-32.

these claims should be confused with fundamental principles of physics which are those that ultimately describe reality.

Similarly, when we ask, "What is the aim of justice?," we could answer that it is to devise principles to regulate the institutions of society that are justifiable to others. If we ask, "What are the methodological constrains on justice?" We might say that we should utilize ideal theory to construct a choice-model to test theories of justice against one another. And finally, if we ask, "What are some virtues of fundamental principles of justice?" We might say that there are many, and include: the "formal constraints on the principles of right,"[326] the idea that principles should generate agreement, and that they should be realistically utopian and feasible for us.[327]

As we can see, none of these answers are properly "fundamental principles of justice," even if some might be fact-free and sit at the summit of our normative convictions. To be sure, we might disagree about these more basic elements of justice, just as there is disagreement about whether simplicity is a true virtue of scientific theories. But we should not confuse disagreement about virtues or methodology with disagreement about fundamental principles of justice. As such, Cohen's argumentative strategy fails to dethrone Rawls's principles of justice from their status as fundamental

---

[326] These are: generality, universality, publicity, capability of ordering claims, and finality. See TJ, 112-118.
[327] We may compare this approach with Rawls's own description in *Justice as Fairness* where he describes the "Four Roles of Political Philosophy," which are: (1) to formulate the moral basis for agreement to resolve deep conflicts, (2) to "orient" ourselves within society and understand ourselves as having a "certain political status," (3) to reconcile ourselves to the world and "accept and affirm" society positively, and (4) to provide a basis for hope through developing the idea of a realistic utopia. See JF, 1-5.

principles. It merely serves to highlight all the different justificatory elements and reasons that underlie them.

Leaving Cohen's more grand strategy behind, we can now consider other arguments that challenge Rawls's use of facts to determine his principles of justice. Briefly though, it is important to emphasize the limited scope of the arguments presented against Cohen thus far. I have not demonstrated yet that facts *should* be included in our determination of principles of justice. I have only shown that Cohen's Socratic method of questioning fails to unearth the true fundamental principles of justice. In other words, the current section addressed the following objection: *If* you rely upon a fact to justify a principle of justice, you must also acknowledge a fact-free principle that is a more fundamental principle of justice. I resisted that conditional argument. In contrast, the next sections will address a different criticism: *Why is Rawls even relying on certain facts in the first place to justify principles of justice?* And so, the following discussion will be devoted to addressing specific challenges to Rawls's use of facts, including the "circumstances of justice," facts about human nature, and facts related to the stability requirement on our conception of justice.

III. Rawls and the Relevance of Facts

Empirical facts play a diverse role in the overall structure of Rawls's work and in his justification of his principles of justice. They are generally appealed to in three separate domains: first, facts play a role in determining when concerns of justice even arise in society--called the circumstances of justice; second, facts appear in the Original

Position (and 'disappear' behind the veil of ignorance) in order to justify the principles of justice over alternative conceptions; and third, facts appear in the final stage of argument when Rawls tests his principles of justice for stability. I will begin with a discussion of the circumstances of justice before considering the other stages of Rawls's arguments for the principles of justice in which facts play a role.

(a) The Circumstances of Justice

According to Rawls, "the first principles of justice depend...on the rather specific features and limitations of human life that give rise to the circumstances of justice."[328] The circumstances of justice are those features that are preconditions for the problem of justice to arise in a society. These are not features that determine what the *content* of the principles of justice are, but rather, features that determine when justice itself emerges.

Rawls states that his understanding of the circumstances of justice does not depart much from David Hume's treatment of the idea in his *Treatise of Human Nature* and the *Enquiry Concerning the Principle of Morals*, so it is natural to begin with Hume's discussion. [329]

---

[328] KC, 351.

[329] However, Rawls does expand upon the idea to include the fact of reasonable pluralism and the burdens of judgment. See TJ, 110 and JF, 84. Rawls also divides his discussion into the "objective" and "subjective" circumstances of judgment, TJ, 109-110. With respect to Hume, there are also two points of difference worth mentioning. First, Hume regards justice as a virtue of persons rather than of institutions. Second, for Hume, justice is fundamentally about respect for the rules of property and for promise-keeping. However, for Rawls, justice is fundamentally about setting the rules for institutions that are necessary for social cooperation. Hence, the circumstances of justice are those preconditions that make social cooperation possible. See Hume, David. *An Enquiry Concerning the Principles of Morals*, ed. by L.A. Selby-Bigge, Oxford Clarendon Press, 1975. Hume, David. *A Treatise of Human Nature*, ed. by L.A. Selby-Bigge, Oxford Clarendon Press, 1978.

(i) Limited Resources and Moderate Scarcity

The first feature among the circumstances of justice is the existence of limited resources, or moderate scarcity. Before justice can arise, there must be sufficient resources to meet the needs of persons. However, resources cannot be so plentiful such that there are no genuine conflicts of interests between people. For instance, if resources poured from the sky like manna from heaven, or if persons could merely extend their hands into an infinite wellspring of nectar and ambrosia to satisfy their thirst and appetite, there would be no need for principles of justice to determine the rules of property. People would simply take what they required without the need to assert ownership to one another. As Hume asks: "Why call this object *mine*, when upon the seizing of it by another, I need but stretch out my hand to possess myself of what is equally valuable?"[330]

One might object that certain things like Shakespearean Sonnets would require rules to protect them even in a state of abundance, since one could not acquire something of 'equal value' in nature. Hence, we might still require rules to govern resources generated through "artifice," even if we did not require rules to govern purely natural resources such as food, water and shelter. A possible reply could be that either that nature was so abundant as to naturally produce objects of wonder that satiated our artistic needs, or that the value of taking a Sonnet from another person would be close

[330] Hume (1975): 184.

to zero, for one would have no reason not to share the sonnet with you, assuming it is infinitely reproducible.[331]

Instead of an absolute abundance of resources in society, we many next consider whether justice would apply if there was an extreme dearth of resources. In this scenario, we are to imagine "such want of all common necessities, that the utmost frugality and industry cannot preserve the greater number from perishing, and the whole from extreme misery."[332] Here, neither nature nor the fruits of cooperative activity would sufficiently provide for the necessities of life. In this scenario, the rules of property would appear to be fruitless, for there would be no disposition to follow them. Whatever it was that people needed in this state of scarcity would simply be taken. For instance, in a shipwreck, people are generally regarded as entitled to take whatever property that was left behind in order to ensure their survival.[333]

Some philosophers, such as Brian Barry, have criticized Hume's circumstances of justice as improperly setting the preconditions of justice with respect to scarcity.[334] Barry argues that, even within a condition of extreme scarcity where resources could

---

[331] Some lingering problems might persist when dealing with resources such as *time*, which, even in a state of pure abundance would be a *cost* placed upon us if we had to take the time to extend our hands to reclaim more food if someone took it from you. And we may care about time because we suffer from eventual bodily death that even a great abundance could not counteract. A strategy here would either be to stipulate that time was also in great abundance (we are immortal), or that the time required to replace any lost resource would be close to zero.

[332] Ibid., 186.

[333] See Hope, Simon. "The Circumstances of Justice," *Hume Studies* vol. 35, no. 2 (2010): 130.

[334] See Hope (2010): 129, for a deeper exploration of these issues. See Barry, Brian. *Theories of Justice*. Harvester-Wheatsheaf, 1989. Also see Nussbaum, Marta. *Frontiers of Justice*. Belknap Press, 2006: 157. Nussbaum argues that justice arises "whenever human beings are around," and that the need to realize human capacities is always important, irrespective of whether scarcity exists. See Hope (2010): 131 for a fuller account of this objection.

not satisfy the basic needs of persons, there could still be principles of *rationing*.[335] For instance, if society were facing a famine or a drought, there could still be restrictive principles that prevented people from simply taking whatever it was that they needed. This is because people recognize that maintaining the rule of law would outweigh the chaos that would ensue if societal rules governing property broke down.

Another analogy one could make to illustrate this point is to examine the problem that hospitals face when allocating scarce resources to persons who need organs. Patients recognize that there are insufficient organs to meet the needs of all; and yet, we do not generally see patients attempting to steal organs from others or jump the queue when their time runs out. Rather, patients themselves recognize that there are binding social rules to determine who gets treatment first, even in conditions where patients stand to suffer or die. Using these examples, one could argue that Hume's circumstances of justice are incorrect, for there are, in fact, problems of justice that arise even within conditions of extreme scarcity.

Simon Hope's reply to this worry is to state that these examples are simply "special cases" that arise in society, and are not genuine examples of scarcity that Hume had in mind. Hope argues: "to make Hume's point clear, we must imagine the *entire domain* of agents facing potential death."[336] So, instead of a local or temporary scarcity, we should imagine that the entire world was impoverished such that no social

---

[335] Barry (1989): 155-56. See also Hubin, Clayton D. "The Scope of Justice," *Philosophy and Public Affairs* 19 (1979): 3–24, 9–10. As quoted in Hope (2010): 129.
[336] Hope (2010): 129.

cooperation or efficient distribution could forestall the immediate threat of death. It is in *this* scenario where no rules governing the institution of property would arise. People would simply take whatever they could find, wherever they could find it.

Some may still be unconvinced by this line of reasoning. Utilitarians, for instance, may argue that, despite the extreme scarcity, there can still be an *inequality of pain* that members can suffer in this cruel state of affairs. We might think, for example, that an adult should nonetheless distribute and prioritize resources to children or others who were sick or injured. On this view, while it might be true that everyone stands to suffer and die, it does not follow that anything goes. There would still be constraints on our behavior that relate to the distribution of pain and suffering.

In reply, we should note that neither Hume nor Rawls believes that justice is the only constraint on our behavior. Hume, for instance, holds that persons still have *natural virtues* such as benevolence that may constrain what people do to one another, even during times of scarcity. For example, if I notice someone at a dried-up river securing one final cup of water to quench his thirst, I may naturally be unwilling to pry the cup from his hands, even if I needed water myself. This unwillingness would be explained by natural virtues, rather than by considerations of justice, and would be the only limiting constraint on my behavior.

To provide another example, Rawls may argue that we have duties of rescue if we happen to find ourselves in favorable circumstances to help another. Rawls says we have "the duty of helping another when he is in need or jeopardy," so if we see that someone is trapped underneath a tree, and will die unless we help her out, we may be obligated to do so, even if we need to continue hunting for food.[337] And, by parity of reasoning, this would not be required out of respect for justice, but because of the existence of natural duties.

(ii) G.A. Cohen's Challenge

Despite this division between natural duties and justice, G.A. Cohen still objects to Rawls and rejects that justice would fail to apply or emerge in cases of extreme scarcity.[338] In fact, Cohen does not believe that the circumstances of justice have any meaning whatsoever with respect to what justice requires. Cohen employs two tactics in his challenge to Rawls. First, he attempts to describe a situation under extreme scarcity where justice would nevertheless apply. Second, Cohen argues that it is always possible to describe the requirements of justice, independent of any factual circumstances that make it impossible or unlikely to be realized.

First, let us examine Cohen's example. According to Cohen:

> There *is* a rule that respects the general conception [of justice] under extreme scarcity, to wit, some sort of (deliberatively contrived) lottery. It may be that most people would be unwilling to introduce that rule or sustain it or submit to it under scarcity, but that does not make the rule impossible. Consider what Rawls might say of that rare and powerful someone who could have seized the only life preserver but who instead rolled dice to determine who would get it, and who had the power to enforce his will, which is to say to impose a just, because equal-chances,

[337] TJ, 98. Rawls also adds a caveat: "provided that one can do so without excessive risk or loss to oneself." It is debatable whether conditions of extreme scarcity would always invalidate the natural duty, but I do not see that it would be the case in all circumstances. My inability to hunt for a brief period of time, even though it is necessary for my survival does not seem to be severe enough to prevent me from helping someone in need.

[338] See Cohen (2008): 331-336.

> structure. *Would Rawls say only that he was amazingly generous? Would he not also say, should he not also say: what a just man he was, to impose an egalitarian structure to his own detriment, under those conditions?*[339]

Cohen's strategy here is to argue that extreme scarcity does not make it impossible for someone to realize a duty of justice, which, for Cohen, means to ensure an "equal-chances" distribution. If someone were to stumble upon some food and decide to cast lots for it to ensure that everyone had an equal chance to eat it, what should we say of that person? Cohen believes that this person is realizing justice in the world—he is not just expressing the natural virtue of beneficence. In fact, the truly beneficent thing to do would be as follows: Suppose, after the lots were cast, this person decided to give the life jacket away to someone else. In this scenario, justice would have already been fulfilled, and so any further action would be supererogatory.

There are various responses we can make to Cohen here. First, by arguing that justice is simply the requirement to realize an "equal-chances" distribution of resources, Cohen is adopting a view of justice that departs from Rawls's understanding of the idea. Through his example, we find that Cohen believes that justice applies *whenever a distribution of resources is at stake*. And since there are still resources that some people get and others do not in conditions of extreme scarcity, justice will enact a judgment upon how those resources are distributed.

---

[339] Cohen (2008): 333, emphasis added.

Rawls, in contrast, does not share this "allocative" view of justice.[340] Rawls believes that "a distribution cannot be judged in isolation," and that we must know the relevant background structure by which resources are produced.[341] For instance, we will need to know of "any existing cooperative relations" that determined the production of goods.[342] Otherwise, "there is simply no answer to this question" regarding what the just distribution of resources is.[343] Merely appealing to the needs and desires of the individuals is not sufficient for determining the requirements of justice. Other principles might be appealed to in order to address meeting the needs of others absent any social cooperation, but justice is not one of them.

Rawls's resistance to an allocative view of justice is connected to his view that "justice is the first virtue of social institutions," and that "the primary subject of justice" is "the basic structure of society."[344] On this view, principles of justice are to apply to institutional structures and not to the individual choices of persons. One of the primary reasons for this insistence is that justice is about the social relations that exist between persons within a set of economic, political, and social institutions. Justice does not concern our relations to human beings as such, or to all persons in the world. The natural duties cover our relations with other persons, and the principles of mutual aid and assistance apply to societies across the world. As such, principles of justice will only

---

[340] TJ, 77: "Allocative justice applies when a given collection of goods is to be divided among definite individuals with known desires and needs."
[341] TJ, 76.
[342] TJ, 77.
[343] TJ, 76.
[344] TJ, 3.

apply in cases where those special cooperative relationships exist that are mediated through institutions.

Given these two considerations about justice—that it is not allocative (it is *relational*), and that it primarily applies to institutions—what can we say about that "rare and powerful someone" who decides to cast lots for the last life preserver in Cohen's example? On Rawls's view, it does not make sense to call that remarkable person a *just* person on the grounds that he realized the principle of "equal-chances" in the world. Instead, one option might be to argue that what the person did was supererogatory since he is benefitting others at great cost to himself.[345] However, a more plausible response is possible. I believe that Rawls would argue that the principle of casting lots could be a valid principle to adopt, but it would not count as a principle of justice, and instead would fall under a moral or ethical category.[346] As such, we may call the person a moral or ethical person, as his behavior would respond to the moral demands of how we treat others independent of our institutional relationships. We cannot, however, deem his behavior as "what justice demands," as there is no special relationship of social cooperation that can exist without institutions in conditions of extreme scarcity.[347]

---

[345] See Rawls's brief discussion of supererogation at TJ, 100: "Supererogatory acts are not required, though normally they would be were it not for the loss or risk involved for the agent himself."

[346] An alternative principle might also be a "first come, first served" principle as the most appropriate principle to adopt in cases of extreme scarcity, absent other confounding variables such as the existence of children. It may depend upon the circumstances of the choice-situation.

[347] There may be limits on even our natural duties as well in conditions of extreme scarcity. At some point, even the moral duties may break down.

Now, Cohen, aware of the "basic structure objection," tries to preempt it by building into his example the fact that the person has "the power to enforce his will" and impose a just "structure" on society.[348] Hence, we are to understand the example as one in which a person could forcibly generate institutional structures that would require the casting of lots for all resources. But this is a poor attempt at satisfying the core of Rawls's objection. If I, for example, had the absolute power to impose an institutional structure on society that complied with the difference principle, this would *not* be justice-serving. Justice is not about enforcing one's will on others to comply with the difference principle, even if that principle were the correct principle that should apply to the institutional framework of society. The institutional structures that are in place must also be "stable for the right reasons," and must be justifiable to others on terms they can accept.[349] One person usurping power to impose one's will on others through the creation of institutions, even if benevolent, would fail these requirements. It would be difficult to see how these institutions would be deserving of our support and allegiance if they did not arise politically and with reinforcing support from citizens. They would most likely deteriorate shortly after being imposed, rendering the exercise of one's powerful will fruitless.

We can now move to Cohen's second objection to the relevance of extreme scarcity for the circumstances of justice. Recall that Cohen uses his life-preserver example to provide a counterexample to Rawls's insistence that, in conditions of

---

[348] Cohen (2008): 333. Cohen indeed argues that this is his intention in the example.
[349] PL, xlii.

extreme scarcity, justice would not emerge. However, Cohen's second tactic is to argue that, even if justice could *never* be satisfied due to extreme scarcity, our knowledge of justice would still be the same—and it would still rightfully "apply" and condemn unjust circumstances. Cohen states the following two claims: "It will always be possible to characterize a situation as either just or unjust: it's false that the question will sometimes fail to apply."[350] Continuing, he argues:

> Even if, and contrary to what I have argued, there could not *be* Rawlsian justice under extreme scarcity, it would not follow that Rawlsian just rules for such circumstances could not be described, and it therefore would not follow that we could not describe such circumstances as productive of injustice.[351]

Cohen's claim here is that, even if extreme scarcity makes it impossible for Rawlsian justice to be realized, justice would still condemn any distributions that failed to realize the difference principle. In other words, even if there could not be any remarkable person who had the will to enforce a just distribution, it would not change the fact that justice still requires a particular distribution to be realized. It may be unfortunate, on Cohen's view, that no one is able to realize justice, but we can still conceptually label the resulting state of affairs as "productive of injustice."

Cohen is essentially implying that justice is like any other conceptual label we might utilize. Consider, for instance, the label "green." If I am describing the clouds, the fact that clouds can't be green does not prevent us from being able to say that "green is not being realized in the clouds." In other words, the fact that something cannot be

---

[350] Cohen (2008): 334.
[351] Ibid., 334.

green does not inhibit our ability to label something as failing to achieve greenness. And likewise, with justice, we can describe a state of affairs as "failing to realize justice," even if that state of affairs cannot realize it, especially in conditions of extreme scarcity.

Only a brief reply is in order here, as I will discuss a version of this objection at a later stage. Cohen is again viewing justice as simply a property of distributions that can be applied anywhere and in all circumstances, rather than as a relational concept that arises within certain institutional parameters that form the basis for social cooperation. In the case of extreme scarcity where institutional rules are impossible, Rawls says that there is simply no answer to the question of what justice requires in terms of distributional requirements. Rawls will *not* say, *pace* Cohen, that the difference principle ought to be the distribution of resources across society in conditions of extreme scarcity, but it is unfortunate that it cannot occur. Instead, Rawls will say that our behavior will now be subject only to moral or ethical constraints as the conditions are now substantially different—there is no possibility for regulative institutions. If the distribution of resources happened to match by mere chance what the difference principle would have required if institutions were in place, Rawls would have nothing whatsoever to say about it. Distributions in and of themselves are simply not relevant to the requirements of justice and the difference principle would not prescribe distributional outcomes on society in the absence of the relevant institutions.

Continuing, I will now leave our discussion of the relevance of scarcity and continue to develop our account of the other feature of the circumstances of justice.

(iii) Limited Altruism

The second feature of the circumstances of justice is the existence of limited altruism. If humans were constructed to be perfect altruists, such that each person's good was contained within everyone else's, there would be no need for an institution of property to demarcate one's possessions from another's; whatever it was that someone needed for his good, another would happily extend it to him if he possessed it, for it would be equally part of his good. As Hume states:

> Suppose, that, though the necessities of human race continue the same as at present, yet the mind is so enlarged, and so replete with friendship and generosity, that every man has the utmost tenderness for every man, and feels no more concern for his own interest than for that of his fellows; it seems evident, that the use of justice would, in this case, be suspended by such an extensive benevolence, nor would the divisions and barriers of property and obligation have ever been thought of.[352]

The central idea is that, since there would be no genuine conflicts of interests in a society composed of perfect altruists, justice would never need to be "thought of" to resolve them.

On the other hand, if persons were so selfish such that they lived in a "society of ruffians" who exhibited such "a disregard to equity, such contempt of order, such stupid blindness to future consequences" that social cooperation would be impossible, people would simply take whatever it was they needed to pursue their own aims.[353] Persons in such an unfortunate state of affairs would only "consult the dictates of self-preservation

---

[352] Hume, David. *An Enquiry Concerning the Principals of Morals*, Section III, Part 1, "Of Justice." http://www.gutenberg.org/files/4320/4320-h/4320-h.htm#2H_SECT3, (2010, January 12th).
[353] Ibid.

alone."[354] In such conditions, justice would fail to constrain the choices of individuals as they would be unable to see social cooperation and property ownership as possible or available to them. There would be no disposition to follow any of the rules to govern them.

(iv) An Ambiguity About Justice

Cohen raises objections to the condition of limited altruism that are similar to the ones presented in our discussion of moderate scarcity, so we will not rehearse them here.[355] Instead, I wish to draw attention to an important ambiguity in Rawls about the relationship between justice and altruism and whether or not justice would truly fail to apply in a society composed of perfect altruists.

Recall earlier in our discussion of ideal theory that Rawls argues that the principle of utility would more accurately be a principle applicable to "perfect altruists."[356] We discussed the hypothetical scenario in which humans were constructed like bees or ants, and were prosocial to the point of regarding the good of oneself to be equivalent to the good of all. In such a scenario, Rawls argues that the most appropriate principle to guide institutions and behavior would be the principle of utility, as it would best fit their motivational structures.

---

[354] Ibid.

[355] Cohen (2008): 334. Cohen would argue that justice will still condemn society for failing to realize the difference principle, regardless of the inability for persons to be motivated to do so.

[356] TJ, 165.

However, we are now faced with the following dilemma: if society were composed of perfect altruists, and humans were akin to bees or ants[357], we must either say that (a) the principle of utility is the correct principle of justice for them, *or* that (b) justice does not apply. According to the circumstances of justice argument, justice should not apply at all; however, according to Rawls's rejection of utilitarianism, justice *would* apply in such a scenario, but it would be the principle of utility. How shall we resolve this ambiguity?

I believe the correct response to this problem requires us to formulate an answer to the following questions: (1) Would citizens in this society view it as a system of social cooperation? and, (2) Would there be a relevant distinction between the "Right" and the "Good?"[358] The answer to (1) seems to be yes. Bee and ant-like persons would view society as a system of social cooperation, except that the society would be organized around *a single dominant end*—the greatest good of all—rather than a multiplicity of different ends. Because of this, the political community would be similar to a communitarian or perfectionistic one in which the cohesion of the group would be contingent upon a shared conception of the good.

However, we might also think that a society of perfect altruists *could* support persons with a multitude of different ends to pursue. The idea would be that, while pluralism would be accepted, everyone would always be ready and willing to sacrifice

---

[357] Bees and ants are not perfect altruists of course, but they illustrate the point sufficiently for our purposes.
[358] TJ, 392-396.

their own good to enable others to pursue their projects. However, it is difficult to see how it could be genuinely possible for persons to pursue a conception of their own good if it is constantly threatened by the needs of others.[359] The perpetual disruptions would make it particularly difficult to have one's own plan of life, and so the society may agree that the best thing for them would be to organize around a dominant end. The possibility of pursuing one's own rational plan of life would therefore drop out altogether.

Regardless of how we interpret the way in which perfect altruism would be realized, it seems clear that citizens would regard their interactions with others as part of a socially cooperative endeavor to maximize the good. This, however, means that the answer to question (2) seems to be *no*; there would be no relevant distinction between the Right and the Good. They would be synonymous. And given that justice is primarily conceived of as a matter of right, there would be no reason to think that matters of justice would arise in a society of perfect altruists.

If justice is not possible, then how should we make sense of Rawls's claim that the principle of utility would apply to them? The best way to interpret Rawls here is that the principle of utility would not be a principle of justice, but an ethical or moral principle that governs their relations. It would be part of their natural duties toward

---

[359] This is a general criticism of utilitarianism, as it invariably causes us to sacrifice our own good for the good of others that makes it difficult to have our own cohesive plan of life.

others. This interpretation would also explain why Rawls also says that the principle of utility is the "*ethic* of perfect altruists."[360]

Our discussion here has important implications for how we should interpret the circumstances of justice. While most interpretations see them as depicting the necessary conditions for social cooperation (Rawls) or the necessary conditions to develop the disposition to obey rules of property (Hume), we should also add the further justification—namely, to provide the necessary conditions for persons to *recognize a distinction between the Right and the Good* itself.

(v) Recap of Circumstances of Justice

In addition to the aforementioned reasons, the two circumstances of justice—limited altruism and moderate scarcity—rule out the existence of justice in either strongly utopian or dystopian societies.[361] In societies where people are blessed with a limitless abundance of resources or exhibit boundless generosity, or in societies where there exists a paucity of goods and a preponderance of hostile feelings that render cooperation impossible, the "cautious, jealous virtue"[362] of justice would not arise. In this regard, justice itself lies within the domain of a *realistic utopia*. If we are dealing with a utopian society—justice will have no purpose—and if we have a brutally realistic society in which people must largely fend for themselves, justice will be in vain.

---

[360] TJ, 165.
[361] Hope (2010): 129.
[362] Hume, Section III, Part 1, "Of Justice." http://www.gutenberg.org/files/4320/4320-h/4320-h.htm#2H_SECT3, (2010, January 12th).

Put in the context of ideal theory, the circumstances of justice describe "features of the world no plausible conception of justice can idealize away."[363] To attempt to find a basis for agreement in such idealized conditions would be without purpose and would not solve the particular problem of how to devise principles of justice to dictate fair terms of cooperation among free and equal citizens who have an interest in pursuing a rational plan of life and developing a sense of justice. In either utopian or dystopian societies, people will not identify with these stated purposes of justice and will instead employ other normative principles to guide and regulate their behavior, if possible.

(b) Facts in the Original Position

Now that we have discussed the importance of facts which precondition the emergence of justice itself, we can now move on to describe the general facts that are invoked in the Original Position to argue for the principles of justice. The way in which this section is organized is as follows: first, I describe a general account of the facts that are permitted and the rationale behind their inclusion or exclusion; and second, I describe facts about human nature and their importance for understanding Rawls's project. I conclude by responding to objections by G.A. Cohen and David Estlund.

<u>(i) Justification for Inclusion and Exclusion of Facts in the OP</u>

One of the most prominent places where facts are discussed with respect to the justification of principles of justice occurs within Rawls's discussion of the original

---

[363] Hope (2010): 126.

position and the veil of ignorance. [364] The original position is a model, or hypothetical standpoint, that represents the appropriate conditions in which representatives of free and equal persons rationally deliberate about the principles of justice for society. The "appropriate conditions" under which this deliberation should occur are, in part, stipulated by our conception of ourselves as free and equal, and is reflected in the veil of ignorance.

The veil of ignorance notoriously shields parties from significant information about the persons they represent—such as facts about their conception of the good, their class and level of wealth, their talents and personality, and the special circumstances of their society. While we recognize that these facts are important to us, we recognize that this information may bias and distort the selection of the principles of justice. Rawls says: "Somehow we must nullify the effects of specific contingencies which put men at odds and tempt them to exploit social and natural circumstances to their own advantage...In order to do this I assume that the parties are situated behind a veil of ignorance."[365]

Hence, the central idea is that such information, if it were not hidden, would give individuals powerful bargaining power and leverage over other members by enabling them to exploit their natural talents, wealth, and social standing to negotiate better principles for themselves. In this sense, the veil of ignorance is a tool to ensure that the

---

[364] TJ, 15-19.
[365] TJ, 118.

outcome of the deliberations in the original position is fair and not affected by morally arbitrary features.

In addition, the *OP* and the veil of ignorance is said to mirror our conception of ourselves as free and equal.[366] It reflects our freedom in the sense that it represents—as one of our higher order interests—our freedom to pursue and revise a conception of the good. It also reflects our equality by representing each person in the same way—as having the two moral powers and having a fundamental interest in developing them. As such, by imposing a veil of ignorance on the parties, the principles of justice that would result would *truly reflect reasons that stem from our fundamental conception of ourselves as free and equal*—and not contingent features of our society or situation.

From this analysis, we can see that Rawls is primarily concerned with at least two features when determining which facts to include or exclude in our deliberations: (1) achieving *fair* terms of deliberation, and (2) representing ourselves as free and equal. However, this now presents us with a question: Do we need to consult any other facts? Can't parties in the original position determine the correct principles of justice simply from the fact that we are free and equal persons, endowed with two moral powers to pursue a conception of the good and develop a sense of justice? Wouldn't the consideration of other facts be "morally arbitrary" as they would not reflect our fundamental and higher order interests?

[366] TJ, 11.

Rawls's answer to this question is no, and there are two reasons for this. First, Rawls does not believe that we will have a sufficient basis for agreement on principles without additional facts available to the parties. Rawls says: if we abstract too much, "the conception [of the original position] would cease to be a natural guide to intuition and would lack a clear sense."[367] For example, if we did not know that humans required energy to navigate the world and pursue their conception of the good, it is not clear that parties would agree that income and wealth would be part of the bundle of primary goods in need of distribution in society. After all, what would they agree upon instead if they did not know this fact? Or, to provide an example from Kant, our conception of property and the principles that govern it are wholly dependent upon the fact that human beings live on a finite globe in which we must share physical spaces with other beings.[368] Absent this fact about the earth, our conception of property itself would be radically different. As these examples illustrate, Rawls believes that we must consult additional facts in order to provide a sufficient basis for agreement in the original position. Otherwise, our deliberations would be indeterminate.

Second, as we have discussed in our discussion on ideal theory, Rawls believes that the principles of justice selected in the original position must be *stable*. Rawls says:

> An important feature of a conception of justice is that it should generate its own support. Its principles should be such that when they are embodied in the basic structure of society men tend to acquire the corresponding sense of justice and develop a desire to act in accordance

[367] TJ, 120.
[368] For a discussion of this point, see Guyer (2013): 178-179. Perhaps this might be a fact to be included under the circumstances of justice.

> with its principles. In this case, a conception of justice is stable. *This kind of general information is admissible in the original position.*[369]

According to Rawls then, if we do not have facts available to us to test for stability, the hypothetical exercise in the original position would be futile, *as it would not solve a central problem of justice*, which is to find principles that citizens can endorse and affirm. It is a pointless task to derive principles of justice based solely on a conception of freedom and equality alone without any knowledge as to whether such a conception of justice would be able to gain the support of persons. Hence, we need to consult additional facts to make the stability test determinate.

What kinds of facts are needed to generate a sufficient basis for agreement and to test for stability? Rawls says:

> As far as possible, then, the only particular facts which the parties know is that their society is subject to the circumstances of justice and whatever this implies. It is taken for granted, however, that they know the general facts about human society. They understand political affairs and the principles of economic theory; they know the basis of social organization and the laws of human psychology.[370]

We can see clearly from this statement that there are three categories of facts that Rawls believes are permitted in the original position: (1) facts that "give rise to the circumstances of justice," which we have already discussed, (2) facts produced by the empirical sciences about the world and the workings of society, and (3) facts about

---

[369] TJ, 119.
[370] TJ, 119.

human nature and human psychology.[371] It is these facts about human psychology and human nature that are the most important for the stability test.

However, it is important to note that these facts must be *general* facts, and not particular facts about specific human beings or societies. We do not test the principles of justice based on each person's unique psychology or personality.[372] Instead, the original position only contains general facts about human beings and societies as such. This is to ensure that parties in the original position do not exploit these facts for their own advantage when selecting principles. To illustrate, if I know, for instance, that I have a cunning personality, I will attempt to use this information as leverage when it comes to debating which liberties I should afforded, or how resources should be distributed. I might argue, for example, that the difference principle is unnecessary for me since my cunning nature would allow me to deceive others into attaining higher positions of power in society. As a result, Rawls denies particular psychological facts about persons in the original position, but allows general facts.

In contrast, we do not typically think that knowledge of general empirical laws generates objectionable biases in our reasoning about what fair terms of social cooperation are, or what rights and liberties we think people should be afforded. This is because these laws *apply to everyone equally*. Of course, we know that scientific laws may lead to eventual harm or misfortune to specific persons—say, lightning striking a

[371] We may perhaps merge (2) and (3) under the umbrella of "facts of the general sciences," but I will proceed as if they are separate for organizational purposes.
[372] Rawls calls these "special psychologies," TJ, 464.

tree and falling on you, or the genetic lottery dealing you a deleterious mutation that causes significant disease—but the point is that we do not know *who* will be harmed or benefitted from these general laws; the veil of ignorance shields this information from us. It is in this sense that the general facts are tolerable in the original position—their *effects* upon us are unknown, and so we cannot use them for our particular benefit. [373]

A further restriction imposed on the general facts available to persons in the original position is that they must be *publicly accessible*. According to this "publicity condition," the principles of justice and their full justification must be transparent to all persons in society.[374] All persons must be able to *discern the reasons* upon which the principles of justice are based, and they must understand and have *access to the facts* that determine the selection of these principles.

The explanation for the publicity condition is threefold for Rawls. First, if citizens are to be coerced through sanctions imposed by the basic institutions of society, then the principles that organize them should be publicly available as a way of justifying that coercion. Otherwise, people will challenge and reject those principles, leading to instability. Second, social institutions have a significant role in determining how citizens shape their wants, desires and aspirations. In order for people to adequately plan and

---

[373] Interestingly, it may be possible to abstract away from certain scientific facts about the world even further than Rawls imagined we could and still reliably agree to Rawls's two principles of justice in the original position. For example, it is not clear that Rawls needs to appeal to the law of gravity anywhere in his reasoning to justify the equal basic liberties, or the priority of liberty over fair equality of opportunity and the difference principle. Nor is it evident that he would need to appeal to the ideal gas law. Nevertheless, these speculations are unnecessary risks for Rawls's goals. Since these facts do not taint the deliberations of the parties in any way, there is little point in abstracting away from them if doing so would increase the possibility of making rational agreement more difficult or less accessible to all.

[374] For a discussion of the publicity condition, see KC, 536-539.

take responsibility for their conception of the good, people must have the ability to assess and evaluate the principles that regulate their institutions that have a significant impact on their plan of life; and third, Rawls believes that it is a "precondition of freedom" to have knowledge about the rules and principles that govern social life.[375] What Rawls means by this is that, if the justification of principles were not sufficiently public, then the maintenance of society would depend upon "delusions" or an "ideology" of "false consciousness" to support them.[376] This would be an unacceptable basis for our principles and would not yield a suitably stable conception of justice. To summarize, Rawls says:

> If institutions rely on coercive sanctions...and influence people's deepest aspirations, the grounds and tendency of these institutions should stand up to public scrutiny....Publicity ensures...that free and equal persons are in a position to know and to accept the background social influences that shape their conception of themselves as persons, as well as their character and conception of their good.[377]

Putting all these conditions together, we can now claim that the facts that are permitted in the original position are the following: (1) facts that express our commitment to freedom and equality, (2) facts that do not create unfair bargaining power between citizens, (3) facts that are relevant for the stability test regarding the principles of justice, (4) facts that are publicly accessible, and (5) *general* facts about human nature, the empirical sciences, and human societies.

---

[375] KC, 539.
[376] Ibid., 539. See fn. 4.
[377] Ibid., 539.

With these conditions, Rawls believes that he will be able to provide a sufficient basis for agreement on principles of justice that reflect his commitment to a realistic utopia. It is realistic in the sense that he allows facts to constrain our principles based upon human nature and the empirical world; however, it is utopian in the sense that he employs a moral conception of the person as free and equal as a starting point, and aims to show how principles of justice can be chosen that reflect this normative ideal. It is *realistically utopian* in the sense that these principles of justice and the moral ideal on which they are based are *compatible and feasible for us* given facts about who we are and the world in which we live.

In the following sections, I will now answer a series of objections by various philosophers who have rejected Rawls's reliance upon facts to argue for principles of justice, including objections by G.A. Cohen and David Estlund.

(ii) G.A. Cohen's and David Estlund's Challenge to the Stability Condition

According to G.A. Cohen, Rawls's concern with stability is misguided and is irrelevant for our understanding of justice. Cohen states:

> To treat the evident desideratum of stability as a constraint on what justice might be thought to be, to judge that principles qualify as principles of justice only if, once instituted, their rule has a propensity to last, is absurd.[378]

Cohen provides two central arguments for this claim. First, Cohen does not believe that the stability requirement allows us to make sense of the *fragility* of justice, and that the following utterance would be nonsensical: "'This society is at the moment just, but it is

[378] Cohen (2008): 327.

likely to lose that feature very soon: justice is such a fragile achievement.'"[379] He thinks this is true because stability is built into the very idea of justice itself: "it is true by definition that there is no danger that justice won't last. And that is absurd."[380]

In order to reply to Cohen's criticism, we need to separate two different states of affairs: *the well-ordered society*, and the *non-ideal world.* In the well-ordered society, it is true that justice is stable. This is part of its appeal to us. However, this does not mean that there will not be *threats* to it—partial tendencies to injustice will inevitably occur due to the burdens of judgment, and other limitations of human nature. For instance, Rawls recognizes the real possibility that "an intolerant sect comes to exist within a well-ordered society."[381] However, Rawls believes that there will be internal mechanisms in society that will aid in the conversion of the intolerant sect to becoming a tolerant one. Rawls says: "This persuasion works on the psychological principle that those whose liberties are protect by and who benefit from a just constitution will, other things equal, acquire an allegiance to it over a period of time."[382]

In other words, the intolerant sect will come to see, through time, the benefits of liberty and will eventually come to acknowledge it as a principle of justice. Hence, what makes a well-ordered society stable, for Rawls, is the following: "Stability means that when

[379] Ibid., 328.
[380] Ibid., 328.
[381] TJ, 192.
[382] TJ, 192.

tendencies to injustice arise, other forces will be called into play that work to preserve the justice of the whole arrangement."[383]

Despite these equilibrium forces, Rawls would certainly recognize that the well-ordered society is *not immune from dissolution*. Significantly unfavorable circumstances may make it simply impossible for it to survive. For example, a series of natural disasters may disrupt the workings of institutions, weakening their effects on the psychologies of the future generations of children who may not grow up to see the benefits of them. Since a society depends upon its future generations to witness and experience the reasonableness of just institutions, if this is made impossible for a long enough period of time, the future generations will likely be set back and unjust institutions may arise. As such, it is quite possible for citizens in the well-ordered society to proclaim that "justice is such a fragile achievement." It is not, *pace* Cohen, "true by definition that there is no danger that justice won't last." Citizens would recognize that well-ordered does not mean that it is *guaranteed* to remain so, and that the uncertainties of the world may conspire against its persistence.

Despite some fragility to the well-ordered society, the power and force of Rawls's conception of justice derives from the fact that it is not *so fragile* that it ceases to motivate us or provide us with genuine and reasonable hope *in the non-ideal world*. When a society is thrown into disarray and chaos, we can know that, when the dust settles, and nature's forces finally wane, the well-ordered society will still stand as a

[383] TJ, 193.

beacon of hope that can unshakably serve to motivate and ease our frustrations with the unpredictability of the world. This is because we recognize that it is, at its core, compatible with our fundamental interests and our moral conception of ourselves. In the right favorable circumstances, and with enough perseverance, it is fundamentally achievable for us.

As such, the citizens in the non-ideal world recognize the difficulty of achieving justice, and would assert the following claim: *injustice is very robust.* They recognize that the steps required to achieve justice will be met with numerous false starts and disappointments. However, they would simultaneously assert that justice is *also very robust.* If it were not, and if it was viewed as fundamentally fragile as to be essentially brittle, it would lose its value and importance for us. We would see no reason to aim for it or strive to realize it.

We can now turn to Cohen's second criticism of the stability condition. Cohen states the following:

> To reject a presumptive principle of justice *precisely* and *solely* because it is unworkable (as a rule of regulation) is to endorse it *as* a principle of justice...Why does Rawls assign a defect to that conception of justice...rather than to people's moral capacities? Is it an axiom that human beings are *capable* of justice? Is 'original sin' a contradiction in terms?"[384]

Here Cohen asserts that, if we recognize a principle of justice to adequately reflect all of our considered convictions about justice, but *only* fails the stability test, we should thereby conclude that we have found the true principle of justice and that *it is our*

---

[384] Cohen (2008): 330.

human nature that is flawed. After all, if such a principle adequately gives shape to our moral conception of ourselves, why would we reject it simply because it was incompatible with human nature? Why isn't the correct response to condemn our nature and bemoan its frailty?

Recall that one main reason for the rejection of utilitarianism was that it failed the stability test—it was shown to be incompatible with our moral motivations in that we could not expect citizens to adhere to its mandates over time. The implication of Cohen's view would then be the opposite conclusion: Instead of condemning the principle, we ought to condemn the human race for failing to be a society of bees with a hive-mind psychology.

David Estlund voices a similar criticism of Rawls's reluctance to criticize human nature's imperfections.[385] Estlund argues that it is part of our normative framework to condemn features of ourselves that we find abhorrent and that Rawls's reliance upon human nature to influence our stability judgments is mistaken. Estlund argues:

> "Rawls's doctrine...silences concerns about whether some motivational structures—however much they might be part of our natures—might be justice-tainting rather than justice-shaping."[386]

To illustrate his point, Estlund argues that Rawls's method forces us to make the following absurd argument:

---

[385] Estlund, David. "Human Nature and the Limits (If Any) of Political Philosophy," *Philosophy and Public Affairs* vol. 39, no. 3 (2011): 207-237.
[386] Ibid., 227.

> People tend to a certain degree of cruelty, and this is part of what they are motivationally like as a matter of human nature. (Suppose this is so.) Therefore, requirements to be otherwise are specious and false.[387]

On Estlund's view, Rawls must allow the parties in the original position to have access to this information when they test the principles for stability. As such, we might find the requirement to secure the equal basic liberties for all persons to be utterly infeasible for human beings because their cruelty would make it motivationally difficult for them to endorse it. They would recognize their desire to dominate and subjugate others, and so they would not accept a principle that required them to deny their basic human nature.

As a final blow to Rawls, Estlund then asks us to consider a hypothetical problem of envy and its potential "justice-tainting" properties.[388] Estlund says:

> Suppose that it is part of human nature that people who recognize their own superior talents will tend to resent and envy people who are, owing to the operation of social institutions, as well-off as they are but without as much talent and ability.[389]

Estlund believes that, if this were true, the difference principle would generate too much envy among the talented and gifted, and so it would be rejected. In such a hypothetical case, Estlund believes that Rawls's methodology would instead recommend principles of justice that "apportion the distribution of social goods according to levels of talent and ability" and that this would then "constitute perfect social justice."[390]

---

[387] Ibid., 224.
[388] Also see Tomlin, Patrick. "Envy, Facts and Justice: A Critique of the Treatment of Envy in Justice as Fairness," *Res Publica* 14, 2008: 101-16.
[389] Estlund (2011): 226.
[390] Ibid., 227.

Given these problems, Estlund concludes that "it is *never* a feature's status as characteristic of humans by nature that constrains the concept of justice,"[391] and that "the rules and institutions that should be constructed given what is known about everyone's likely compliance are hardly guaranteed to be rules and institutions that qualify a society as just."[392] As such, Estlund believes we should reject the stability test if it permits us to illegitimately smuggle in objectionable features of human nature into our determination of principles of justice. Estlund believes we have *independent moral reasons* for criticizing or affirming these motivational features of human nature. We can, for instance, condemn the selfishness or the narrow-mindedness of human psychology rather than resign oneself to it at the level of fundamental normative principles. While the application of these principles must take these features into consideration, the utmost peak of our normative framework should steer clear from them.

Cohen corroborates Estlund's position in his final pithy remark:

The flesh may be weak, but one should not make a principle out of that.[393]

(iii) Rawls's Reply to Cohen and Estlund

My reply to these criticisms will be separated into two parts. First, I will argue that the features of human nature that we find most problematic—our tendency toward cruelty, envy, or our desire for power and domination over others—are actually "special psychologies" that we do not have good reasons to believe would exist in dangerous

[391] Ibid., 228.
[392] Ibid., 226.
[393] Cohen (2008): 173.

levels in the well-ordered society.[394] As such, we would not permit them in the original position as a basis for the selection of our principles of justice. In the second part, I will argue that Rawls does have the tools to criticize features of human nature if it turns out that humans would be so disfigured as to be truly unfit for justice in Rawls's sense.

Let us begin with the first claim, that the special psychologies will not exist to a large extent in the well-ordered society, and that they should also not be included in the original position. According to Rawls, "a rational individual is not subject to envy, at least when the differences between himself and others are not thought to be the result of injustice and do not exceed certain limits."[395] Rawls also says that the "various tendencies to dominate or to submit" will also be mitigated for similar reasons.[396] The central argument for this conclusion is that many of our beliefs about our basic psychological attitudes are actually the result of injustice in the world, and are likely to fade away under just institutions.[397]

To illustrate, Rawls argues that a well-ordered society governed by the difference principle would not largely consist of individuals with strong desires to accumulate more wealth. Rawls states that the desire for wealth typically results "from insecurity and anxiety," and that "to the extent that just institutions alleviate these

---

[394] TJ, 464.
[395] TJ, 464.
[396] TJ, 464.
[397] This reply reminds us of Rousseau's criticism of Hobbes when he accuses Hobbes of projecting the malformed and destructive psychologies of citizens onto the person in a state of nature. For Rousseau, it was the fact that people were raised under disfigured societal institutions that caused people to manifest destructive tendencies. Hobbes mistook these tendencies to be part of our fundamental nature, and so his description of the state of nature was mistaken. See Rousseau, Jean-Jacques. "Discourse on the Origin of Inequality," in *Classics of Moral and Political Philosophy*, ed, by Steven M. Cahn, Oxford University Press, 2012: 547-548.

psychological conditions, they reduce the strength of the quest for wealth and position."[398] As such, we do not have reasons to believe that these desires are *general features of human beings*, or even if they were, they would not be so pronounced as to pose a threat to the stability of our institutions. Hence, Rawls argues that we should not allow the parties in the original position to be affected by them.

However, even if we challenged Rawls on this point, Rawls also argues that including the special psychologies in the original position would pose a further problem for the deliberators. At the very least, there would be great uncertainty as to how much persons would be affected by them. Rawls says, "without rather definite information about which configuration of attitudes existed, one might not be able to say what agreement if any would be reached."[399] Given this problem, we must "avoid the complications in the bargaining process that would result."[400] And so, "for reasons both of simplicity and moral theory, I have assumed an absence of envy and a lack of knowledge of the special psychologies."[401]

---

[398] See Rawls, "Fairness to Goodness," CP, 277. Rawls can also employ this argument to respond to Cohen's criticism that the difference principle allows for profit-maximizing marketeers to flourish in the well-ordered society. Rawls can reply that, because of certain psychological mechanisms and dispositions of people, this will not likely occur. See Cohen, G.A. "Incentives, Inequality and Community," *The Tanner Lectures on Human Values,* vol. XIII, ed. by G.B Peterson. University of Utah Press, 1992. Also see Cohen, Joshua. "Taking People as They Are?" *Philosophy and Public Affairs* Vol. 30, No. 4 (2001): 363-386.

[399] TJ, 465.

[400] TJ, 465.

[401] TJ, 465. However, Rawls does allow a consideration of envy in the stability test, *after* the principles of justice are chosen. Rawls believes that there does exist the possibility of "excusable envy" in persons if the disparity of wealth between persons was so great that the worst-off would regard their self-respect as damaged. Rawls says: "A person's lesser position as measures by the index of objective primary goods may be so great as to wound his self-respect: and given his situation, we may sympathize with his loss," TJ, 468. Rawls continues saying that this envy is "not irrational," and that if "the principles of justice are likely to arouse so much excusable envy,"

We can also frame Rawls's point in another way. Recall that one of the limitations on the facts allowed in the original position is that they must satisfy the publicity criterion. If there would be no consensus on the general facts about our liability to envy or other special psychologies, we cannot appeal to them. As such, it would be preferable to withhold them from the parties, for otherwise the full justification for the principles of justice would not be available to all persons.

However, one worry for Rawls's strategy here might be that our criteria for what should be included as a special psychology is now too stringent. Could we not argue that *all claims about human nature are controversial and liable to be part of a special psychology*? And if so, how could we justify relying upon any claims about human nature at all? To provide some plausibility to this, consider the range of views from prominent biologists as well as philosophers of science about the matter.

According to Michael Ghiselin:

> What does evolution teach us about human nature? It tells us that human nature is a superstition.[402]

And David Buller argues:

> The idea of a universal human nature is deeply antithetical to a truly evolutionary view of our species...A truly evolutionary psychology should

---

then "the choice of these principles should be reconsidered," TJ, 468. We should compare this with what Estlund is asking us to imagine. Estlund is asking us to consider people with so much envy that they resent those who do not have to work as hard for their income. I do not believe that Rawls would think that this kind of envy will be very pronounced. People are given responsibility for their ends in society and are able to choose their own rational plan of life. If people were "envious" of those who did not have to work very hard, *they would have the choice and opportunity* to change their life plan and revise their life accordingly, with the full guarantee that their basic liberties and fair opportunities would not dissipate.

[402] Ghiselin, Michael. *Metaphysics and the Origin of Species*. SUNY Press, 1997: 1.

> abandon the quest for human nature and with it any attempt to discover universal laws of human psychology.[403]

And finally, Tim Lewens argues:

> Many philosophers of biology today think about human nature in the same way that they think about race. Race is commonly regarded as having no basis in biological reality, and the same, it is sometimes said, goes for human nature.[404]

This is, of course, not the place to engage in these extensive debates. However, I believe Rawls can largely deflect these more skeptical views about human nature when we consider what Rawls actually includes when he discusses the general facts about human nature.

Let us examine, for instance, the sense of justice which is perhaps the most central psychological capacity that human beings have, as it includes the capacity for reciprocity, which entails tit-for-tat motivations and "a tendency to answer in kind."[405] According to Rawls:

> A capacity for a sense of justice built up by responses in kind would appear to be a condition of human sociability....Beings with a different psychology either have never existed or must soon have disappeared in the course of evolution.[406]

---

[403] Buller, David. *Adapting Minds: Evolutionary Psychology and the Persistent Quest for Human Nature*. MIT Press, 2005:419.

[404] Lewens, Tim. *Cultural Evolution*, Oxford University Press, 2015: 61.

[405] TJ, 433. The sense of justice contains both a normative and empirical component. It is part of our conception of the person, but it is also compatible with our moral psychology and our psychological attitudes. This is how Rawls views the interaction between the conception of the person and human nature. Rawls says: our moral conception of the person is "limited by the capacities of human nature," and that "such an ideal presupposes a theory of human nature," KC, 534.

[406] TJ, 433.

In other words, Rawls argues that the very foundation for social cooperation as we know it rests upon human beings having a capacity for reciprocity. Otherwise, coordination would not be possible for us and societies as we know them would not exist. Rawls also invokes the theory of evolution to explain how persons who cooperated with a sense of justice were more likely to form stable unions that persisted over time than those groups who did not.[407] He even argues that social groups that had more utilitarian psychologies could not be stable for "its members would risk domination" by other social groups that would emerge to take advantage of their universal benevolence.[408]

Of course, Rawls merely stating these features of human psychology does not make them true, as they are largely empirical conjectures.[409] However, the level of skepticism about human nature in general should not be understood to apply to these more basic elements that are viewed as preconditions for our capacity to view society *as a system of social cooperation based on reciprocity*. If this turned out to be false, the entire conception of justice would need to be entirely recast. As Rawls states:

> A person who lacks a sense of justice lacks certain fundamental attitudes and capacities included under the notion of humanity....there is no way

[407] TJ, 433.
[408] TJ, 441.
[409] Rawls does offer additional arguments for the empirical development of the sense of justice. Rawls believes that his conjectures for how the sense of justice could develop is consistent with Jean Piaget's work in developmental psychology regarding the development of the moral feelings in children. He cites in CP, 100, fn.5: Piaget, Jean. *The Moral Judgment of the Child*. Routledge, 1932. Rawls argues that we can understand the development of the sense of justice by appealing to various forms of guilt that are implicit in our relations with others—particularly between our family members—as well as between members of our associations. See CP, 100-106.

> for us to avoid a liability to them [moral feelings] without disfiguring ourselves.[410]

As such, we cannot plausibly suspend judgement upon these features of human nature, as they are intricately connected with our moral conception of ourselves as being fundamentally *reasonable* creatures capable of restraining our behavior based on considerations of reciprocity. To deny this about ourselves would be to say that humans are not, in fact, capable of justice as we know it at all. Hence, Rawls argues:

> It is hard to imagine realistically any new knowledge that should convince us that these ideals are not feasible, given what we know about the general nature of the world.[411]

Consequently, for Rawls, there is little reason to be skeptical of these more general features of human nature.[412]

This completes the first stage of my reply to Cohen and Estlund. The central idea is that we should not expect the special psychologies of envy or the desire to dominate others to be destabilizing forces in the well-ordered society, and that there are certain empirical generalizations of human nature that are plausible for Rawls to appeal to in the original position to argue for the stability of principles of justice.

We must now turn to the second stage of my reply, for Cohen and Estlund are also making a much *deeper* criticism of Rawls's reliance upon facts related to stability, human nature and feasibility to argue for his principles of justice. Their argument is not

---

[410] CP, 112

[411] KC, 566.

[412] Rawls does say that we can accommodate new knowledge, however. Rawls believes that "advances in our knowledge of human psychology and social theory might be relevant at the constitutional, legislative, and judicial stages in the application of the principles of justice, as opposed to the adoption of principles in the original position." KC, 566, fn. 15.

simply that envy or cruelty might taint the principles of justice *in our world*. Rather, it is the stronger claim that we would not be able to condemn it as a flaw of human nature if it turned out to be endemic to human life in some other possible world. As Estlund argues, if, *hypothetically*, human beings were so envious of others that they could not tolerate the difference principle, we should not acquiesce to the frailty of human nature and revise our conception of justice. We should instead condemn it as an utmost affront to justice. It is this more radical claim that I must reply to now.

Implicit in both Estlund's and Cohen's criticism is that our conception of justice can be "hopelessly" unattainable if it turns out that human nature is not up to the challenge to meet its demands.[413] However, Rawls makes the opposite conclusion. Rawls does not believe that a conception of justice must always be a slave to our more demanding moral ideals about what kinds of creatures we *ought* to be. Rawls says:

> A political conception must be practicable, fall under the art of the possible. This contrasts with a moral conception that is not political: a moral conception may condemn the world and human nature as too corrupt to be moved by its precepts and ideals.[414]

So, Rawls does acknowledge that human nature may be judged to be fundamentally corrupt or morally bankrupt. However, these pronouncements must be a part of our conception of the good and cannot be a part of the political realm. The reason for this is because a conception of justice must be fundamentally achievable for us. It is part of Rawls's vision of a realistic utopia that our conception of justice is possible and capable

---

[413] For a discussion of the relevance of "hopeless" theories of justice, see Estlund, David. "Utopophobia" *Philosophy and Public Affairs* vol. 42, no. 2 (2014): 113-134.
[414] JF, 185.

of generating agreement among reasonable and rational persons. If our conception of justice itself condemned human nature, it would not be possible for persons to rationally agree upon it. After all, what purpose would it serve other than to make it impossible to "reconcile" ourselves with the world?[415] How could we expect persons to develop the requisite motives to affirm it without trouncing upon the freedom of others?[416]

And so, to answer Estlund's claim about envy, if it were *hypothetically possible* that human beings were too envious of others to endorse the difference principle, the principles of justice would have to be recast. Again, Rawls vehemently denies this possibility[417], and it would only be a theoretical exercise.[418] And, since it is only a theoretical point, it should have no bearing on the thoroughly practical components of justice.

However, there is one caveat to Rawls's claim here, and Cohen and Estlund may take solace in his words:

> If a reasonably just society...is not possible, and human beings are largely amoral, if not incurably cynical and self-centered, one might ask with Kant whether it is worthwhile for human beings to live on the earth.[419]

---

[415] JF, 1-5.

[416] I am thinking here of the doctrine of original sin. Many societies, of course, have attempted to base social relations upon it. However, the only method by which one could do so would be through an unreasonable limitation on the freedom of thought and the liberties of others who might not share such a view. Hence, reasonable agreement would not be possible.

[417] See my fn. 150 for a further defense of this claim.

[418] Rawls admits that his Kantian Constructivism allows for the *theoretical* possibility for his principles of justice to change if the general facts about human nature were to be radically different. However, Rawls only "regard[s] this as a mere possibility noted in order to explain the nature of a constructivist view." See KC, 566.

[419] LP, 128.

It might seem as if Rawls is contradicting himself in these two statements. After all, shouldn't Rawls concede that, if human beings were entirely selfish that different principles of justice should apply to them? Principles that, in a sense, "fit their nature?"

Rawls's answer here is that, if human nature does not even afford the basic materials to allow humans to be governed by the reasonable, it would be pointless to attempt to constrain their behavior by justice. The sense of justice would not exist in these persons, and it would therefore be impossible for all persons to be able to pursue their conception of the good in this world with any degree of security. Such persons would forever live in fear of others and would likely die alone and in misery. Such a world would be akin to Hobbes's state of war, in which life was "solitary, poor, nasty, brutish, and short."[420] In *this* world, Rawls would join the chorus of Cohen and Estlund, condemning the miserable fate of humanity, for it would turn out that the higher-order interests of all persons would be permanently left unfulfilled and no principles of justice could ever be affirmed to secure them.

However, if Rawls's empirical musings and conjectures are at all accurate, our worry about whether such humans would be fit for the earth would quickly be answered—Rawls believes such beings would quickly die out as their capacity for social life would be impossible. The forces of evolution would eliminate them from the earth, sparing us the thought of such unfortunate creatures.

---

[420] Hobbes, *Leviathan*, in *Classics of Political and Moral Philosophy*, ed, by Steven M. Cahn, Oxford University Press, 2012: 393.

To answer Cohen's claim then, if the flesh is weak, our conception of justice will likely mitigate those weaknesses; if the flesh is still weak, we may need to revise our principles of justice; but if the flesh is *too weak*, then such creatures would not be fit for justice and would not be long for this world.

Chapter 6: Embracing a Hopeful Ideal

I. Resisting Hopeless Ideals

David Miller, in the conclusion to his book, *Justice for Earthlings*, urges us not to succumb to the idea of "political philosophy as lamentation," according to which the task of political philosophy is to cling to hopeless ideals in defiance against the world.[421] Miller's target is the political philosophy of the late G.A. Cohen, as well as David Estlund, who both assert in differing degrees that the demands of justice are independent of our flawed human nature, our corrupted society, and the circumstances of the world which make justice fundamentally infeasible for us. According to this philosophical orientation, all facts about human nature and society are contingent and morally arbitrary distractions that prevent us from fully grasping the true essence of justice which resides in a "Heavenly City," never to be reached by mere mortals such as ourselves.[422] In contrast, the "Earthly City," where imperfect human creatures reside, should be lamented and condemned for failing to realize the high demands of justice from above, perpetually reminding us of our frailty and fundamental weaknesses.

According to Miller, such a view of the world is a "pathological" response to our shaken and defeated moral aspirations when confronted with the realization that there is no place on earth in which such aspirations can be fulfilled.[423] Instead of relinquishing

---

[421] Miller, David. *Justice for Earthlings*. Oxford University Press, 2013: 228-249.
[422] Miller borrows the idea of the Heavenly City and the Earthly City from Augustine's *City of God* in which Augustine argues that justice could never be achieved in the earthly city, and that it resided in the City of God instead. Miller (2013): 228-230.
[423] Ibid., 230-231. Miller argues that this response for Augustine was to the fall of Rome, and for G.A. Cohen, to the collapse of the Berlin Wall in 1989.

these ideals, we project them, unscathed, onto a distant utopia. By placing these ideals forever out of reach, we, in a final effort to forestall defeat, "rescue justice and equality" by enshrining them in a timeless and sacrosanct city, never to be ransacked or destroyed again.

Miller believes that this escape now turns political philosophy into a "purely speculative activity,"[424] detached with concerns of feasibility and achievability, and tainted with undertones of resignation, lamentation, and perhaps even resentment. Consider the almost iconic statement from Cohen:

> The question for political philosophy is not what we should do but what we should think, even when what we should think makes no practical difference.[425]

And so, we think, contemplate, and muse on perfect justice. If our penetrating thoughts reveal that justice condemns the world and humanity, that is to be our fate; we are forever bound to its demands. Here is Cohen, again:

> In believing that justice must be so crafted as to be bottom-line feasible, they believe that it is possible to achieve justice, and I am not so sanguine. It follows from my position that justice is an unachievable (although a nevertheless governing) ideal.[426]

David Estlund supports Cohen's outlook and defends an approach to political philosophy which he calls "hopeless aspirational theory," according to which justice "defends standards even though they will *not* be met, and even if we knew this for sure."[427] Continuing, Estlund argues that truth is the governing ideal for justice, just as it is in

---

[424] Ibid., 232.
[425] Cohen (2008): 268.
[426] Ibid., 254.
[427] Estlund, David. "Utopophobia," *Philosophy and Public Affairs* vol. 42, no. 2 (2014): 118.

"pure mathematics," and that its practical value is of secondary importance.[428] While Estlund does believe that hopeless theories *can* have practical value, justice, nevertheless, is a theoretical exercise that is grounded in "curiosity,"[429] and if it turns out to have absolutely no practical value, justice remains what it is, unaffected by its impossibility and inapplicability for us. Estlund states:

> Even if (as I doubt) understanding justice would have no practical value, and even if (as I doubt) for that reason, not the kind of thing a person should spend a lot of time on, and even if (as I doubt) such understanding has little or no value of any kind, none of this would show that the truth about justice *is* bound to have practical value. Whether there is any value in knowing about it or not, I have argued that a standard of justice is not automatically shaped so as to guarantee that we ought, given what we know about how we and others will behave in the future, to set out toward achieving it. Looked at the other way around, just because it is not something we ought to set out for does not mean it is not the genuine standard of social justice.[430]

According to Estlund and Cohen, then, we have a standard of justice that is only tangentially related to the practical, and is primarily considered an exercise in theoretical thought at the highest level of abstraction, unadulterated with factual constraints about feasibility. If these pure concepts of justice end up fundamentally unachievable for us, or provide us with no action-guiding potential, it is no fault of the conception of justice. Instead, it would just be a fact about justice that humans are unable to achieve it and act upon its demands.

---

[428] Estlund (2014): 133-134.
[429] Ibid., 133.
[430] Ibid., 134.

In order to assess Cohen's and Estlund's radical approach to justice, I will investigate two questions: first, in what sense can a hopeless theory of justice, according to Cohen, serve as a "governing ideal," or, according to Estlund, potentially have any practical value (even though it does not necessarily have to); and second, is justice fundamentally a theoretical or a practical endeavor? To answer these two questions, I must first outline what I believe to be Cohen's political methodology that is implicit in much of his work. After doing so, we will see that the action-guiding potential of a purely speculative discipline will not ultimately be fruitful, and that justice should be conceived of as a primarily practical discipline.

(a) Cohen's Method: Intuitionism and Radical Pluralism

G.A. Cohen adheres to a normative philosophical method that he calls, "radical pluralism," or what Rawls would call "intuitionism," which is a method of political philosophizing that consists of identifying a set of irreducibly moral concepts that lie at the foundation of our normative thought.[431] These might be, for instance, Justice, Beauty, Happiness, Prudence, etc.[432] The role of the philosopher, according to this method, is to engage in a thorough-going dialectic to eventually discover what these concepts are, eventually leading to a pinnacle or summit at which no further explication is possible. After discovering what each consists of, we then attempt to apply them to the empirical world to guide our actions and direct our institutions in particular cases.

---

[431] Cohen (2008): 4; TJ, 30-36.

[432] Cohen (2008) pays homage to Plato and Socrates for this approach, p. 291. Rawls cites Moore, G.E. *Principia Ethica* Cambridge University Press, 1903, and Ross, W.D. *The Foundations of Ethics*, Oxford Clarendon, 1939.

However, what is crucial about the intuitionist method is that there is no "higher-order" court of appeals that we can summon in order to weigh these fundamental concepts against one another other should they conflict. Instead, we must rely upon pure "intuition" and clarity of thought.[433] So, when justice and other values conflict, such as efficiency or prudence, it is up to us to determine what best course of action best balances these different demands.

One consequence of this view is that certain moral concepts, like justice, will lack a certain primacy over our other values.[434] As such, Cohen reminds us that justice must give way to efficiency or other considerations when we must design the institutions to regulate society.[435] It is doubtful, then, that justice could ever be fully realized in the world. There are simply too many other valuable considerations that must be accommodated, and it is not possible to simultaneously realize them all at once. So, when Cohen asserts that justice may not be feasible for us, he means that its demands are fundamentally incompatible with other values that must be realized in the world once we are presented with all the facts, which include facts about human beings and social life.

---

[433] TJ, 30. For a longer discussion of Cohen's method, see Vrousalis, Nicholas. *The Political Philosophy of G.A. Cohen: Back to Socialist Basics*. Bloomsbury Academic, 2015: 4.

[434] For a defense of the *primacy* of justice over our personal pursuits, see Tan, Kok-Chor. *Justice, Institutions, and Luck*. Oxford University Press, 2012: 26-32. Also Tan, Kok-Chor. "Justice and Personal Pursuits," *The Journal of Philosophy* vol. 101, no. 7 (2004): 331-362.

[435] Cohen (2008): 302: "I don't see how anyone, whatever she thinks justice is, can deny the possibility that certain facts, or other values, might make it inappropriate, or too difficult, or too costly, to produce justice.

To illustrate, suppose that, upon reflection, we discern that justice demands equality or the neutralization of luck on all distributive outcomes.[436] Cohen absolutely recognizes that this value cannot be fully realized or instantiated in the world—human imperfections and limitations, including our inability to settle the free will problem, all inhibit our understanding and implementation of it. Moreover, the level of state interference in our own personal lives required to realize it will vehemently count against the demands of justice.[437] However, this does not bother Cohen, for he never claims that *we ought to actually implement justice and nothing else*.[438] Instead, we must always be engaged in a balancing act of sorts, weighing and considering on a case by case basis which trade-offs of our values will be best. It is in this sense that Cohen's philosophical method is both radically pluralist and intuitionist: there are numerous values that exist that do not trump the other, and the only way to determine the best course of action is to think about it, test it, and subject it to numerous critical inquiry. The goal is that, at the end of the process, we will end up with a greater clarity with respect to the ultimate question as to what we should do.

We can now answer the two questions that framed our discussion. With respect to the question in what sense hopeless theories can have practical value, the answer is

---

[436] See Cohen, G.A. "On the Currency of Egalitarian Justice," *Ethics*, vol. 99, no. 4 (1989): 906-944.

[437] For a critique of luck egalitarianism on the grounds of institutional infeasibility, among other serious problems, see Anderson, Elizabeth. "What is the Point of Equality?" *Ethics* vol. 109, no. 2 (1999): 287-337.

[438] Cohen (2008) says: "Difficulties of implementation, just as such, do not defeat luck egalitarianism as a conception of justice, since it is not a constraint on a sound conception of justice that it should always be sensible to strive to implement it, whatever the factual circumstances may be. Justice is not the only value that calls for (appropriately balanced) implementation: other principles, sometimes competing with justice, must also be variously pursued and honored," p. 271-272.

that they figure indirectly in our ultimate normative calculus when deciding the "all-things-considered" best course of action.[439] While the institutions we build in society may fail to fully implement justice, they are still directed and shaped in some way by its mandates. Regarding the second question, the search for justice is primarily theoretical in the sense that it aims to provide a clear understanding of the concept of justice *first*, independent of the contexts in which it is to be applied, before turning to the question of *how we should act practically*. These two inquiries are distinct, and one concerns purely matters of belief and thought, and the other, norms for action.[440]

(b) Rawls's Criticism of Intuitionism

Rawls views his contributions in *A Theory of Justice* as a response to the kind of intuitionist theorizing endorsed by Cohen.[441] Rawls is primarily unsatisfied with the radical uncertainty regarding the weighing of different values and principles when they conflict with one another. According to Rawls, "Intuitionism holds that in our judgments of social justice we must eventually reach a pluralism of first principles in regard to which we can only say that it seems to us more correct to balance them this way rather than that."[442] To illustrate, for a luck egalitarian, they must find a way to balance the claims to neutralize luck and to promote efficiency. The hope, is, for intuitionist, that "men will in fact balance them more or less similarly."[443]

---

[439] Cohen (2008): 275.
[440] See Wallace, R.J. "Practical Reason," in *the Stanford Encyclopedia of Philosophy*, https://plato.stanford.edu/entries/practical-reason/ (2014, March 26th).
[441] TJ, 30-36.
[442] TJ, 34.
[443] TJ, 34.

However, Rawls believes that the open-endedness and the limitless number of cases to which these principles must be applied makes this convergence unlikely, and that different conceptions of justice will likely emerge. The result of this is deeply problematic for Rawls, as he says that "the assignment of weights is an essential and not a minor part of a conception of justice. If we cannot explain how these weights are to be determined by reasonable ethical criteria, *the means of rational discussion have come to an end*."[444] In this sense, agreement on principles of justice would not be likely, and the problem of justice will then not be adequately solved.

Rawls seeks to solve this problem by limiting the role of intuition and allowing it to operate in a more confined and restricted domain. He does *not* believe that we can eliminate altogether the role of intuition in our normative judgments. Indeed, Rawls says that the goal of justice as fairness is "reducing and not of eliminating entirely the reliance on intuitive judgments. There is no reason to suppose that we can avoid all appeals to intuition."[445] Instead, the goal should be to determine a method by which we can more clearly and fruitfully appeal to our intuitions and *generate a basis for agreement*.[446] Rawls accomplishes this task in three ways.

First, Rawls constructs the original position to provide greater clarity and impartiality to our intuitions. The veil of ignorance, more specifically, prevents our own circumstances from clouding and biasing our intuitive judgments. One major source of

[444] TJ, 37.
[445] TJ, 39.
[446] TJ, 39: "The practical aim is to reach a reasonably reliable agreement in judgment in order to provide a common conception of justice."

disagreement in how to apply our intuitions is due to the disparate effects circumstantial facts have on our intuition. Rawls eliminates this source of disagreement through the imposition of the veil of ignorance. In addition, Rawls allows parties knowledge of general basic facts to shape our intuitive judgments. If we did not supply reasoners with the general circumstances of justice and basic facts about human beings as such, including an account of their fundamental and higher-order interests, the task of finding principles that could generate agreement would be near impossible. Rawls states his case against intuitionism in the following powerful paragraph:

> Some philosophers have thought that ethical first principles should be independent of all contingent assumptions, that they should take for granted no truths except those of logic and others that follow from these by an analysis of concepts. Moral conceptions should hold for all possible worlds. Now this view makes moral philosophy the study of creation: an examination of the reflections an omnipotent deity might entertain in determining which is the best of all possible worlds. Even the general facts of nature are to be chosen. Certainly we have a natural religious interest in the ethics of creation. But it would appear to outrun human comprehension. From the point of view of contract theory it amounts to supposing that the persons in the original position know nothing at all about themselves or their world. *How, then, can they possibly make a decision?* A problem of choice is well defined only if the alternatives are suitably restricted by natural laws and other constraints...Without a definite structure of this kind the question posed is indeterminate....If these assumptions are true and suitably general, everything is in order, *for without these elements, the whole scheme would be pointless and empty.*[447]

Rawls's statement here expresses the importance of establishing the materials necessary for agreement. If we are to merely concern ourselves with our intuitive

---

[447] TJ, 137-8.

concepts in isolation, our musings will be indeterminate and may not yield conclusive judgments about what we ought to do.[448]

Interestingly, and perhaps to Cohen's relief, Rawls says that "there is nothing intrinsically irrational about this intuitionist doctrine. Indeed, it may be true."[449] However, Rawls does not regard "truth" to be the goal for justice. Instead, justice is about finding *reasonable* principles that are capable of being agreed upon to govern our institutions and determine how rights and resources are to be assigned and distributed.[450] As such, our intuitive judgements must be restricted and clarified in order to produce the basis for public agreement. Otherwise, we will not have solved the problem of justice.

For this reason, Rawls does not regard the principles of justice to be "self-evident" or foundationalist in our thinking in the same way that our pure intuitions might be.[451] Because the principles of justice are the result of a choice-situation in which our intuitive judgments are considered against one another in a limited fashion, it is difficult to see in what sense justice might be self-evidently true. In fact, it would be quite

---

[448] Thomas Pogge expresses a similar criticism of Cohen's methodology when he says, "I can say that I find it absurd, and morally offensive to extend my moral principles to beings and life contexts that I have not experienced and do not really understand," and that "Cohen does not explore, let alone engage, the reasons there might be for modesty about the range of one's moral principles." See Pogge, Thomas. "Cohen to the Rescue!" *Ratio* 21, no. 4 (2008): 467, 469.

[449] TJ, 35.

[450] To be clear, *that* justice is about finding principles capable of agreement to govern the assignment and distribution of rights and social goods is supposed to be a truth about the "*concept* of justice." The *principles* of justice, however, are not to be regarded as theoretical truths, and form the "*conception* of justice." See TJ, 5 and TJ, 9.

[451] TJ, 37: "In justice as fairness the principles of justice are not thought of as self-evident." However, Rawls also thinks that these intuitions may change in reflective equilibrium. Rawls says, "even the judgements we take provisionally as fixed points are liable to revision," TJ, 18.

difficult to arrive at the principles of justice without the original position procedure, for otherwise our convictions would be muddled and indeterminate.[452]

In addition to allowing general facts and imposing a veil of ignorance in the original position, Rawls also limits the choice-situation in the original position by "substituting prudential for moral judgment."[453] By stipulating that the parties in the original position are to be governed by the principles of rational choice,[454] we further limit the role of our intuitive moral judgements about how we should distribute resources and assign rights and liberties. By stipulating an account of the primary goods that any rational person can be seen to want, and describing persons as having two fundamental capacities—an interest in pursuing and revising a conception of the good and developing a sense of justice—we can adopt prudential reasoning to determine which principles would be selected to best safeguard these interests. If we allow other forms of reasoning into the deliberation, such as moral reasons that stem from a conception of the good, our agreement will again be indeterminate.[455]

Finally, Rawls limits the role of intuition in our determination of principles of justice by providing a list of conceptions of justice to select from that have been developed in our philosophical legacy. Of course, Rawls admits that, "ideally one would

---

[452] For a disagreement about the necessity of the original position procedure to arrive at Rawls's principles of justice, see Scanlon, Thomas. "Contractualism and Utilitarianism,' in Amartya Sen and B. Williams, *Utilitarianism and Beyond*, Cambridge University Press, 1982: 103–128.
[453] TJ, 39.
[454] These include, taking "the most effective means to one's ends," and to prefer more of a good than less, etc., JF, 85, and TJ, 123—130.
[455] For instance, Rawls imagines someone who is religious or an ascetic who may, for moral reasons, not desire to have more primary goods at all. See, TJ, 123.

like to say that they are to choose among all possible conceptions of justice."[456] However, it is simply not available to us to know with any clarity what these full conceptions of justice would look like without them first being developed into a concrete framework. In the future, if other conceptions are fully articulated, they may be considered as alternatives, but it makes no sense to consider partial or undeveloped accounts.[457]

Taking all these conditions into account, (1) the construction of the original position, (2) the description of the parties as rational,[458] and (3) the limited selection of conceptions of the justice, we are now able to build a "framework designed to focus our moral sensibilities and to put before our intuitive capacities more limited and manageable questions for judgement."[459] It is Rawls's belief that, only in such a confined choice situation can we determine principles of justice and assign the appropriate weights to our different intuitions—such as deriving the priority of liberty over the desire for an increased number of primary goods.[460]

With Rawls's methodology outlined, we can now return to the two questions posed to Cohen and Estlund and offer a criticism of their answers. First, with respect to the question of what practical value a conception of justice would have if it were part of

---

[456] TJ, 105.
[457] Rawls does allow mixed conceptions, which are different for they have been more fully developed in our political and economic relations with others. However, Rawls does acknowledge that these are much more difficult to evaluate. See, TJ, 277-285.
[458] We may also add that the parties are "mutually disinterested" in order to avoid problems of representatives wanting to be altruistic towards others. See, TJ, 125.
[459] TJ, 46.
[460] I do not have the space here to produce the entire argument for the principles of justice and their priority. However, this section suffices to demonstrate how Rawls believes that we must limit our reliance on intuition to make judgments about the ultimate requirements of justice.

a pure intuitive judgment that was independent of all facts and limiting conditions, Rawls's answer would be that it would have very little practical value, for there would be no way to determine what its recommendations would be for how we should fundamentally regulate our basic institutions. This is because an intuitionist account of what we should "all-things-considered" do would unlikely generate agreement about how best to balance and weigh the various values and principles against one another. For, according to what metric would these disputes be resolved? The intuitionist methodology has no other answer than to recommend a retreat further and further into a theoretical cocoon with the hope that a more definite answer can be provided. As such, the prospects for practical proposals to be reached to guide the design of our institutions becomes much more challenging and haphazard. To be sure, *it can be done* in the sense that *some* decision can be made by some particular person—but whether or not that decision can be *justified to all members* and *agreed upon* is another matter altogether and should be the ultimate goal of justice.

Rawls's solution, alternatively, is to condense the space in which these judgments may be pursued, preventing the unending retreat into the limitless theoretical space in which these Forms of Justice and other values operate. In doing so, we open the possibility for agreement on practical principles to govern our institutions.

Regarding the second question, to what extent political philosophy is a theoretical or a practical exercise, Rawls would reiterate that the primary concern for justice is to find reasonable principles that persons can agree upon. The question of truth is either inapplicable to justice, or, more modestly, best left to a conception of the good. Given the impossibility of an agreement on these more controversial and limitless interpretations of our intuitive judgments, they cannot serve as a public criterion by which to navigate and frame our social relations with others. While there may be some "truth" to the matter to be found in the deep speculative libraries of the Heavenly City, it is not likely to be an ideal to which citizens can endorse for all. It is, after all, unlikely that each person would engage in the "ethics of creation" in the same manner.

With these criticisms in place, we may now return to Miller's diagnosis of Cohen's outlook on political philosophy. Despite Cohen's "rescue" of justice and equality and the attempt to enshrine these concepts in a pristine and flawless city, this rescue of justice is really an imprisonment, a Trojan Horse designed to sabotage and hijack our normative outlook. For now, instead of inspiring us and motivating us to rectify the wrongs of the earth, we are left with an account of justice that can only be contemplated and eternally refined. When we try to act upon it, we are left with an indeterminate muddle of conflicting claims that can only serve to paralyze and frustrate our aims and aspirations. Without any possibility for agreement, we can only retreat into the greater confines in our minds, clinging onto our ideals of justice and remaining in a permanent state of *aporia*, wondering if the world will ever live up to its demands.

It is perhaps Miller's psychological thesis that this *aporia* leads to condemnation and lamentation of the world.[461] The idea would be that a permanent inability for

---

[461] The exposition here is my own and I only mean to suggest that it is in the spirit of Miller's analysis.

humans to realize justice in the world *must* have some connection with our moral psychology and our attitudes. If our conception of justice is such that it remains forever out of reach—that luck can never ultimately be neutralized, or that we can never live in a perfectly socialist society[462]—our psychological reaction to this perpetual failure of justice must be devastating for us and a source of unrelenting sorrow. There would be truly no hope for us, no matter our best efforts; the Earthly City would forever be a mere shadow of true Justice and should be mourned, and ultimately condemned. Such an assault on our moral psychology is bound to leave us disfigured and debilitated.

Cohen has three possible responses to this line of thought. First, he could reject the connection between violations of justice and the changes in our moral attitudes and emotions. After all, if justice is, as Estlund and Cohen claim, purely a *theoretical* concept akin to the "curiosity" of "pure mathematics,"[463] why should it have any relationship to our moral emotions whatsoever?

However, this would only serve to highlight the strangeness of Cohen's view. By relying upon a theoretical concept of justice, he now cannot provide us with an account of *any* moral emotions at all. For, while mathematical truths may invoke a sense of wonder or amazement, or may even generate frustration when we are unable to unfold

---

[462] Cohen, in his book *Why not Socialism?* argues that the feasibility of socialism should be a separate question from the desirability of socialism itself as an ideal of justice. Cohen himself admits ambivalence about the feasibility of socialism for us, but he asserts that this fact should not deter us from stating that the ideally just society is one that is purely socialist in nature. Cohen, G.A. *Why not Socialism?* Princeton University Press, 2009.

[463] Estlund (2014): 133. Adam Swift makes a similar argument in Swift, Adam. "The Value of Philosophy in Nonideal Circumstances," *Social Theory and Practice*, vol. 34, no. 3 (2008): 363-387.

their deepest mysteries, *these are not moral emotions.*[464] Consequently, if justice is purely a theoretical concept that does not necessarily connect with moral attitudes, then it is difficult to see why we should *care* that much about justice outside of its theoretical interests. It would be just one among many other values that compete in a timeless and unending struggle with other ideals in the realm of theoretical reason.

This reply should also serve as a sufficient answer to Estlund's attempt to save hopeless theories of justice by claiming that they can still have value in the way that pure mathematics can. While it is true that theoretical justice in this sense could still provide value, *it is not the right kind of value that we require from a concept of justice*. We need a concept that allows for the relevant engagement with the moral emotions—not one that is limited to theoretical wonder and puzzlement. Our failings of justice must evoke resentment.[465] If they did not, we would doubt that we genuinely regarded them as unjust in the first place. As such, the study of justice as a purely mathematical or theoretical exercise cannot generate the relevant emotions necessarily connected with injustice.

Hence, if one endorses a hopeless conception of justice as Cohen and Estlund do, then one is faced with a dilemma: either you cannot provide an adequate account of the moral emotions associated with justice, or, even if you could, our moral attitudes

---

[464] This claim is reminiscent, though not perfectly analogous, of Hume's argument that violations of reason cannot be the source of moral principles for they cannot generate the relevant moral emotions. See Hume, David. *A Treatise of Human Nature*, eds. David Norton and Mary Norton. Oxford University Press, 2000: 2.3.3, 265-270.

[465] Rawls argues that resentment is an appropriate response to injustice: "Resentment is a moral feeling. If we resent our having less than others, it must be because we think that their being better off is the result of unjust institutions, or wrongful conduct on their part," TJ, 467.

would be so overwhelmed by the persistent impossibility of achieving justice that they would morph into unhindered resentment and lamentation.[466] Either of these outcomes should be unacceptable to us, for it would entail that our response to the world in the face of injustice should either resemble the attitude of a coolly distant mathematician who discovers a mathematical proof—"Eureka! I have discovered the true nature of injustice!"—or, it should drive us downright *mad*, our emotions flooded with such melancholy and eventual contempt for the world and its inhabitants that we are left with no choice *but* to retreat to the citadels of the Heavenly City to achieve some semblance of calm as we contemplate the peace and happiness that are ultimately possible there.

Faced with this dilemma, I believe that Cohen would assert that our conception of justice should, in some sense, drive us to the brink of insanity.[467] He would insist that the injustices of the world are what they are and anyone with enough clarity of mind should be in a state of perpetual sorrow, dejection, and dissatisfaction. While we may certainly attempt to *correct it,* we can never fully purge its corruption. This is simply the reality of our condition. Anyone who attempts to deny this essential fact is under the grip of a weak and corrupted ideology that seeks to drag down justice into the dirt of humanity. It would be the ultimate delusion to think that justice must somehow answer

---

[466] This dilemma is interestingly similar in one regard to the criticism of utilitarian theories of justice in that they require moral demands upon us that are incompatible with our moral psychology.

[467] In other words, I deny that Cohen would adopt the purely mathematical stance in which judgments of justice should be met with a sense of discovery or notion of eureka.

to the facts of humanity and our world. Instead, justice condemns it and tells us that our reality is fundamentally a reality of unmet ideals and shattered dreams.

However, is such a moral outlook possible for us? Where is our hope, our relief? Can we be truly and deeply motivated to fix the world if it is ultimately impossible for us to do so? Cohen's vision bears a striking resemblance to the doctrine of original sin and the psychological responses to it.[468] When faced with the judgment that man's nature is fundamentally fallen, many are driven to the religious promise of heaven. It is how many people tolerate a world endlessly marred by injustice and human corruption. Our moral psychology demands some respite from such a wretched judgment and so, it is no surprise that people turn to God and the Heavenly City to provide that salvation for us. And while many are motivated to do God's work on the earth to improve it, ultimate peace and relief are found in heaven, far beyond the capabilities of this world. This is how we achieve some semblance of moral psychological stability.

However, Cohen does not allow for the promise of salvation in Heaven, and nor does he recommend a belief in God to reconcile our fate. And so, we must seek relief elsewhere—our moral psychology demands it. While we might think that we would now have more motivation to fight for a better world without the distraction of Heaven, this does not occur. Now, without the relief from the divine, Cohen instead creates it in our own minds. The Heavenly City now exists in the deep crevices of theoretical and abstract human reason, unspoiled by the rotting prison of the empirical world. Pure

---

[468] Indeed, Cohen questions: "Is original sin a contradiction in terms?" Cohen (2008): 330.

reason then is our new version of God—it is timeless, limitless, and is the only fortress left to provide us with respite in the face of perpetual injustices that cannot end.

And so, Cohen's vision is as follows: We are fundamentally unfit for justice, though we can at least take solace in our discovery and contemplation of *the timeless theoretical truth* of The Just Society. The clarity of mind that is reached in this discovery is its own version of tranquility. As we contemplate the perfect socialist society in which equality reigns and the brute forces of luck are extinguished, we find peace. And while we may be motivated to make the world a better place, as many religious individuals strive to do, *ultimate* peace is only found in the workings of the mind and not through our actions to improve the earth. And there is the fatal flaw of Cohen's approach. Our vision of utopia is not possible for us, and so our motivation to create it on this earth will be motivationally stunted and frustrated. While it is certainly *not impossible* to be motivated to work towards achieving justice, it will be weak and extraordinarily difficult for us to translate those theoretical recommendations into practice. This is because there is no genuine clarity of vision as to how to enact justice in this world. As Estlund reminds us, "actions in pursuit of what will never be achieved [even if it is what justice requires] can be wasteful or even disastrous."[469] And so, what shall we do with our thoughts about justice when we cannot satisfactorily combine them with our other values and the factual constrains of the world? We retreat into our mind and contemplate them once again.

---

[469] Estlund (2014): 120.

While Cohen may think that criticizing the wealthy[470] and condemning the economic incentives necessary to work hard will produce more justice in the world, this only serves to demonstrate the weakness of his mathematical understanding of justice and its detached pronouncements from the Heavenly City of pure reason. For without a hopeful and possible vision of a just society to offer people, these criticisms will fall flat and fail to reliably motivate such persons to relinquish their privileges and accept change. No amount of prophetic demonization of their injustice will create genuine change, for there is no way to connect those criticisms into a vision that people can see enacted in their world.

It is the ultimate irony of ironies that Marx, who condemned religion for its creation of passive individuals with a diminished interest in correcting the injustices on Earth, has now produced an acolyte whose vision of justice creates a similar psychology. It is also surprising that Cohen failed to heed one of Marx's most important dictates, that "the philosophers have only interpreted the world, in various ways. The point, however, is to change it."[471] Cohen's utopia and his purely theoretical account of justice is antithetical to Marx's vision and cannot produce the required conditions necessary to produce genuine and lasting change in the world.

---

[470] Cohen, G.A. *If You're an Egalitarian, How Come You're So Rich?* Oxford University Press, 2000.
[471] Marx, Karl. *Theses On Feuerbach*, XI.
https://www.marxists.org/archive/marx/works/1845/theses/theses.htm (2005, February)

II. A Realistic Utopia Defended

I believe that Rawls's vision can do better. However, he must now answer to the criticisms of those on the other side of the spectrum who subject his vision of a realistic utopia to an intense scrutiny of the same rigor that I have presented against Cohen. According to these critics, Rawls's vision of the just society is simply another inert ideal, incapable of generating real change in the world. Indeed, even if we acknowledge that Rawls's conception of justice is not so far into heaven as Cohen's vision, might it not still be somewhere out of reach for us? It is this criticism to which I must now provide an answer.

At the core of the realist criticism is a great skepticism about the possibility for genuine agreement between persons on a conception of justice. In this regard, realists share a similarity with intuitionists, for both recognize the impossibility of persons to converge on ultimate principles. Intuitionists assert that the world is simply too complex and our judgments too disparate to ever produce agreement on all the fundamental normative values. Rawls says: "The intuitionist believes...that the complexity of the moral facts defies our efforts to give a full account of our judgments and necessitates a plurality of competing principles,"[472] and that intuitionists remind us to "recognize the possibility that there is no way to get beyond a plurality of principles."[473] I have already attempted to respond to this criticism by showing how

---

[472] TJ, 35.
[473] TJ, 36.

agreement is nevertheless possible when we subject our intuitions to the constrains outlined in the original position.

Realists, in contrast, highlight an alternative source of disagreement and skepticism: a less sanguine account of human nature and our psychological motivations. Realists emphasize the deep and perpetual conflicts of interests that are inherent to social and political life, and they do not believe that persons possess the requisite psychological materials to ultimately be guided by Rawls's methodology and vision. For instance, what *actual* motivations do people have to enter into the perspective of the original position? Why would they deny information about their conception of the good when it is fundamental to their identity?[474]

At the core of these criticisms is that *people will simply be unwilling to endorse a conception of justice that does not serve their current interests.* It is simply too much to ask of people to bracket what is most important to them just for the purposes of agreement—they will seek agreement in other ways that are more temporary and short-lived if it means protecting their current interests.

Hence, the original position, while an interesting model for what *hypothetical persons* might agree upon, is not appealing to *actual* persons who are too entrenched by their own conceptions of the good and cannot, in good faith, be asked to set them aside for purposes of fairness. As such, justice must always be a *compromise* between

---

[474] This is the criticism of Michael Sandel (admittedly not a realist, but a communitarian, though I would argue that he shares a similar skepticism of Rawls as realists do). Sandel, Michael. *Liberalism and the Limits of Justice*, Cambridge University Press, 1982.

particular and "contingent" interests people have. Contra Rawls, people do not see a distinction between their fundamental or higher-order interests and their *actual* interests. Persons believe that their *actual* conception of the good is fundamental to them, not their *capacity* to pursue their conception of the good.

And so, justice must retreat from the domain of universal agreement, and descend to the level of bargaining and compromise. *This* capacity—our capacity to strike agreements and bargain with our interests—defines our sense of justice. Rawls's insistence that there is some "deep reciprocity" at the heart of social relations is just another myth and a fiction.[475] Instead, this notion of reciprocity is what Rawls aspires there to be in persons—it is, in other words, an *ideal* of reciprocity, not actual reciprocity as it is realized in the actual world. While *some* persons may possess it and develop it, it is really akin to the distribution of benevolence and altruism in society—it is quite limited and scarce among humanity.

These are deep criticisms of Rawls's vision regarding what human beings can strive to achieve in this world, and they challenge the limits of what persons can be expected to do in the name of fairness. However, I believe that this objection can be answered.

Let me begin with the following uncontroversial claim, and deduce from it what I believe to be the strongest case for Rawls's belief in the possibility of a realistic utopia. That claim is this: The existence of injustice in the world has truly devastating

---

[475] JF, 124.

consequences for us all—not only for those who suffer directly from it, *but also for those who benefit from it and do not incur its most severe costs*. The psychological disfigurement that results in persons who benefit from injustice can, however, be internally felt and acknowledged—it is not something that is imposed on them from a religious ideology or other external doctrine. It may, perhaps, *begin* that way, but it is Rawls's belief that *people can come to internally recognize their own aversion to benefiting from injustice*, and that the cognitive dissonance that results from it will be deeply disconcerting for them. As such, they will be motivated to eliminate it.

If this were not the case, it would be remarkable that any great advancement of justice by persecuted minorities could ever have transpired within liberal democracies. For, without the ability to appeal to the sense of justice of the broader community, their clamors for change would be entirely in vain. This is the lesson of Rawls's account of civil disobedience. We must convince others—particularly those who are in power and are already benefitting from injustice—that living with injustice is intolerable and unacceptable. However, Rawls again believes that our capacity to convince these persons that injustice *cannot be experienced as a good for them* can ultimately come from within, by appeal to our considered convictions that the original position can more clearly manifest for us. And, importantly, the original position is not an external demonstration, but a heuristic engagement with our own considered convictions and our moral sensibilities to allow us to *see for ourselves* that we are benefiting from injustice and that this should cause us deep distress.

One consequence of this approach is that, in societies in which there is no common sense of justice to appeal to, especially in those that are not liberal democracies by any measure, Rawls's conception of justice will have limited application, and an entirely different theory will be required.[476] For in such societies, the need for revolution, violent resistance, or succession may be the best course of action in response to injustice.

However, I must now pause and address a deep objection put forth by those who might find my defense of Rawls's theory of justice to be perverse. For the implication of my defense is the following idea: *A theory of justice is not fundamentally addressed to those who are the victims of injustice, but is instead an appeal to the already powerful and privileged group, in order to get them to acknowledge that living with injustice is a great harm to them.* Doesn't this make the whole idea of justice a concept limited to the privileged?[477] Is this not a deeply offensive notion that a conception of justice *must be fundamentally addressed to those who do not suffer from injustice?*

This is, however, only *partly* true. To be sure, it *does* speak to Sen's criticism of ideal theories of justice as being oddly disconnected with the actual injustices of the world. Sen's question is essentially the following: What *use* is a theory of justice anyway? People already know they are suffering from injustice. We do not need to

---

[476] Rawls began this project in *The Law of Peoples*, but it is inadequate to address these other kinds of deeper problems. But this is not a fault of Rawls, but is only due to the limited time he had on this earth.
[477] See Mills, Charles. "Ideal Theory as Ideology," *Hypatia* vol. 20, no. 3 (2005): 165-184.

construct an ideal theory of justice to demonstrate that to them. We should start working now towards eliminating it.

My response to this objection is the following: Rawls's theory of justice is *for everyone* in the sense that it can serve as the legitimate public criterion of justice that each and every person can endorse and accept in society, no matter what their position or circumstance. However, in terms of *the impact* of Rawls's theory of justice, it is to some extent a redundancy for those who are already suffering. They already *know* their fundamental interests are not taken seriously, and they are deeply aware of the utter damage that has been done to their sense of self-respect and standing in society. Their hurt is real and palpable, and they stand ready to be motivated to act for change. In this sense, a theory of justice will perhaps not motivate them any further. Nevertheless, it will still *answer* and *resonate* with their deepest aims and voiced frustrations. In fact, it may even serve to demolish any false illusions that persons have constructed about themselves who are victims of injustice without acknowledging it. They may have tried to deny the horrible treatment to them in order to save their own sense of psychological integrity and self-respect. A theory of justice may serve to liberate these persons from the psychological damage of self-deception and malformed adaptive preferences.

However, for the powerful and the privileged, Rawls's theory of justice must be utterly transformative if it is to be deemed successful. And on that front, I believe Rawls will be shown to have succeeded, for the basic ingredients of Rawls's theory are within the framework of liberal democratic political life, and are represented in the considered convictions of all persons who regard themselves as free and equal—the powerful included. His vision will eventually work to shape the attitudes of those persons who have the power to reconstruct the basic institutions of society, and it will also influence the powerful to rally behind and speak up for those who have no voice in society. They are already well aware of their grievances, they simply need the influence to make them heard by the entirety of society.

And so, I conclude with two final thoughts: First, realists may respond by arguing that, fundamentally, Rawls's project will fail for human psychology is simply too weak to overcome our natural biases, and that humans will never relinquish their power and resources once they have them secured. The reason for this pessimism is that realists have seen the subjugation, the domination, the brutal and bloodied political arena, and the adamant refusal by the powerful to rectify egregious wrongs. They do not believe that it is any stretch to conclude that these domineering elements of human nature will ever be controlled or eliminated.

However, maybe, just maybe, those who benefit from injustice are not at root too devilish to give up their benefits, but are perhaps simply *fearful* that, in the absence of a realistic utopia, when they relinquish control, they themselves will be the ones who end up being subjected and victimized. While those who are currently suffering from injustice may clamor for this kind of divine retribution against the privileged—*it is their turn now*—this is not the kind of change Rawls believes is at the heart of justice. By constructing a realistic utopia, *all persons* can endorse and be motivated to work towards the establishment of just institutions.

And so, the hesitation by the powerful to vote for policies that divert powers, opportunities, and resources from themselves is actually quite *a natural human response to the desire for a realistic utopia that can be achieved for us.* The reluctance is not due to a devilish desire grounded in selfishness and hatred.[478] Persons mostly desire assurance that their sacrifices are not in vain and merely squandered by society and corrupt politicians with no grand vision for how to transform society. Without some ideal of a well-ordered society that can be shown to be possible for us, no one can be expected to relinquish their opportunities and sacrifice their resources to pursue any haphazard desire to simply do good. Persons are owed a reasonable expectation that their labor be used for purposes that have a deep possibility of lasting success.

The idea of a realistic utopia can provide that vision for us all. A pure or hopeless utopia, in contrast, cannot provide this vision. Persons cannot be expected to comply with judgments from the high citadel that offer *no hope whatsoever for us.* The theoretical pronouncements from pure reason are insufficient and cannot form the basis for a public conception of justice for all reasonable persons. They will invariably fall on deaf ears, for there is no deep connection within it to our moral motivations that desire to see lasting change in the world that is not ultimately in vain.

---

[478] Though for some persons it may appear this way on the surface. However, I would argue that hatred is the result of a long history of failures rather than some innate orientation that persons with power must, by definition, have.

And now a final concluding thought. While a theory of justice shares some similarities with mathematics in its higher abstractions, political philosophy is a humanistic discipline that must answer to our deepest and most fundamental interests that form the conception of ourselves as free and equal human beings. If political philosophy ever diverts from this main focus, its relevance and importance for us will be diluted and its potential to inspire us will vanish.

And so I will leave us with an answer to our initial question of how ideal and utopian we should view Rawls's theory. Is it in the Heavenly City, or does it reside elsewhere? I shall say that the vision of a realistic utopia should reside in the stars. For the stars are *somewhere we can go*, and they are inspiring to us. We acknowledge that they are *deeply difficult* to reach, but they are real enough to keep our motivations intact and steady. Humanity depends on the belief that justice is within reach in order to have a chance at peace—not the kind of peace that is defined by the absence of war, but a kind of internal peace that derives from the recognition that "each person possesses an inviolability founded on justice that even the welfare of society as a whole cannot override."[479] I believe that Rawls would have endorsed this vision for his world.

---

[479] TJ, 3.

BIBLIOGRAPHY

Anderson, Elizabeth. "What is the Point of Equality?" *Ethics* vol. 109, no. 2 (1999): 287 337.

Arrow, Kenneth. *Social Choice and Individual Values*, Yale University Press, 1951.

Barry, Brian. *Theories of Justice*. Harvester-Wheatsheaf, 1989.

Beitz, Charles. "Justice and International Relations," *Philosophy and Public Affairs* 4, no. 4 (1975): 360-89.

Buchanan, Allen. *Justice, Legitimacy, and Self-Determination*. New York: Oxford University Press, 2004.

Buller, David. *Adapting Minds: Evolutionary Psychology and the Persistent Quest for Human Nature*. MIT Press, 2005.

Cahn, Steven M. *Classics of Political and Moral Philosophy*, 2nd edition. Oxford University Press, 2012.

Cartwright, Nancy. *How the Laws of Physics Lie*. Oxford University Press, 1983.

Celikates, Robin. "Civil Disobedience as a Practice of Civic Freedom," in *On Global Citizenship*, by James Tully, Bloomsbury, 2014.

Cohen, G.A. "On the Currency of Egalitarian Justice," *Ethics*, vol. 99, no. 4 (1989): 906-944.

Cohen, G.A. "Incentives, Inequality and Community," *The Tanner Lectures on Human Values*, vol. XIII, ed. by G.B. Peterson. University of Utah Press, 1992.

Cohen, G.A. *If You're An Egalitarian, How Come You're So Rich?* Oxford University Press, 2000.

Cohen, G.A. *Rescuing Justice and Equality*. Harvard University Press, 2008.

Cohen, G.A. *Why not Socialism?* Princeton University Press, 2009.

Cohen, Joshua. "Taking People as They Are?" *Philosophy and Public Affairs* Vol. 30, No. 4 (2001): 363-386.

Dahl, Robert. *Polyarchy*, Yale University Press, 1971.

Dworkin, Ronald. "On Not Prosecuting Civil Disobedience," *The New York Review of Books*, June 6, 1968.

Dworkin, Ronald. *Sovereign Virtue*. Harvard University Press, 2000.

Elkin, Stephen. *Reconstructing the Commercial Republic: Constitutional Design after Madison*, University of Chicago Press, 2006.

Erman, Eva and Niklas Möller. "Three Failed Charges against Ideal Theory," *Social Theory and Practice* 39, no.1 (2013): 19-44.

Estlund, David. "Human Nature and the Limits (If Any) of Political Philosophy," *Philosophy and Public Affairs* 39, no. 3 (2011): 207-236.

Estlund, David. "Utopophobia," *Philosophy and Public Affairs* 42, no. 2 (2014): 113-134.

Farrelly, Colin. "Justice in Ideal Theory: A Refutation," *Political Studies* 55 (2007): 844 864.

Free Exchange, "Making the second best of it," *The Economist*, http://www.economist.com/node/20015054/print (2007, August 21st).

Freeman, Samuel. *The Cambridge Companion to Rawls*. Cambridge University Press, 2003.

Freeman, Samuel. *Justice and the Social Contract: Essays in Rawlsian Political Philosophy*. Oxford University Press, 2006.

Freeman, Samuel. *Rawls*. Routledge, 2007.

Freeman, Samuel. "Constructivism, Facts, and Moral Justification," in *Contemporary Debates in Political Philosophy*, ed. by Thomas Christiano and John Christman, 2009.

Freeman, Samuel. "A New Theory of Justice," *New York Review of Books*, October 14th, 2010.

Freeman, Samuel. "Ideal Theory and the Justice of Institutions vs. Comprehensive Outcomes," *Rutgers Law Journal*, vol. 43, issue 2 (2012): 169-209.

Freeman, Samuel. "The Original Position," *The Stanford Encyclopedia of Philosophy*. https://plato.stanford.edu/entries/original-position/#ArgForDifPri (2014, September 9th)

Gaus, Gerald. *The Tyranny of the Ideal: Justice in a Diverse Society*. Princeton University Press, 2016.

Galston, William. "Realism in Political Theory," *European Journal of Political Theory* 9, no. 4 (2010): 385-411.

Gheaus, Anca. "The Feasibility Constraint on the Concept of Justice," *The Philosophical Quarterly* 63, no. 252 (2013): 445-464.

Ghiselin, Michael. *Metaphysics and the Origin of Species*. SUNY Press, 1997.

Gilabert, Pablo. "Debate: Feasibility and Socialism," *The Journal of Political Philosophy* 19, no. 1 (2011): 52-63.

Godfrey-Smith, Peter. *Philosophy of Biology*. Princeton University Press, 2014.

Goodin, Robert. "Political Ideals and Political Practice," *British Journal of Political Science* 25, (1995): 37-56.

Grenberg, Jeanine. *Kant and the Ethics of Humility: A Story of Dependence, Corruption and Virtue*. Cambridge University Press, 2005.

Guyer, Paul. *Kant*. Routledge, 2006.

Guyer, Paul. "Constructivism and Self-Constitution," in *Kant on Practical Justification: Interpretive Essays*, ed. by Mark Timmons and Sorin Baiasu. Oxford University Press, 2013.

Hamlin, Alan and Zofia Stemplowska. "Theory, Ideal Theory, and the Theory of Ideals." *Political Studies Review* 10 (2012): 48-62.

Hobbes, Thomas. *Leviathan*, ed. by Richard Tuck. Cambridge University Press, 2007.

Hope, Simon. "The Circumstances of Justice," *Hume Studies* 35, no. 2 (2010): 125-148.

Hubin, Clayton D. "The Scope of Justice," *Philosophy and Public Affairs* 19 (1979): 3-24.

Hume, David. *An Enquiry Concerning the Principles of Morals*, ed. by L.A. Selby-Bigge, Oxford Clarendon Press, 1975.

Hume, David. *A Treatise of Human Nature*, ed. by L.A. Selby-Bigge, Oxford Clarendon Press, 1978.

Hume, David. *A Treatise of Human Nature*, eds. David Norton and Mary Norton. Oxford University Press, 2000.

Hume, David. *An Enquiry Concerning the Principals of Morals*. Project Gutenberg. http://www.gutenberg.org/files/4320/4320-h/4320-h.htm#2H_SECT3, (2010, January 12).

Johnson, Oliver. "The Kantian Interpretation," *Ethics* vol. 85, no. 1 (1974): 58-66.

Kant, Immanuel. *Groundwork for the Metaphysics of Morals*. Hackett, 1981.

Kant, Immanuel. *The Metaphysics of Morals*, trans. and ed. by M.J. Gregor, in *The Cambridge Edition of the Works of Immanuel Kant*. Cambridge University Press, 1991.

Korsgaard, Christine. *Self-Constitution*. Oxford University Press, 2009.

Lewens, Tim. *Cultural Evolution*, Oxford University Press, 2015.

Lipsey, Richard G. and Kelvin Lancaster. "The General Theory of the Second Best," *The Review of Economic Studies* 24, no. 1 (1956-57):11-32.

Lipsey, Richard G. "Reflections on the General Theory of the Second Best at its Golden Jubilee," *International Tax and Public Finance* 14 (2007): 349-364.

Lyons, David. "Moral Judgement, Historical Reality, and Civil Disobedience," *Philosophy and Public Affairs* vol. 27, no. 1 (1998): 31–49.

Marx, Karl. *Theses On Feuerbach,* XI. Marx/Engles Internet Archive. https://www.marxists.org/archive/marx/works/1845/theses/theses.htm (2005, February).

Mason, Andrew. "Rawlsian Theory and the Circumstances of Politics," *Political Theory* vol. 38,no. 5 (2010): 658-683.

McShea, Daniel and Alex Rosenberg. *Philosophy of Biology*. Routledge, 2008.

Miller, David. *Justice for Earthlings: Essays in Political Philosophy*. Cambridge University Press, 2013.

Miller, David. *Strangers in Our Midst: The Political Philosophy of Immigration*. Harvard University Press, 2016.

Mills, Charles. "Ideal Theory as Ideology," *Hypatia* vol. 20, no. 3 (2005): 165-184.

Mills, Charles and Carol Pateman. *Contract and Domination*. Cambridge: Polity Press, 2007.

Moore, G.E. *Principia Ethica.* Cambridge University Press, 1903.

Nagel, Thomas. "What Makes a Political Theory Utopian," *Social Research* 56, no. 4 (1989): 903-920.

Nussbaum, Martha. *Frontiers of Justice*. Belknap Press, 2006.

O'Neill, Onora. *Towards Justice and Virtue: A Constructivist Account of Practical Reasoning*. Cambridge University Press, 1996.

Piaget, Jean. *The Moral Judgment of the Child*. Routledge, 1932.

Pogge, Thomas. "Cohen to the Rescue!" *Ratio* 21, no. 4 (2008): 454-475.

Rawls, John. "Kantian Constructivism in Moral Theory," *The Journal of Philosophy* 77, no. 9 (1980): 515-572.

Rawls, John. *Political Liberalism*. Columbia University Press, 1993.

Rawls, John. *A Theory of Justice*, Revised Edition. Harvard University Press, 1999.

Rawls, John. *Collected Papers*, ed. by Samuel Freeman. Harvard University Press, 1999.

Rawls, John. *The Law of Peoples*. Harvard University Press, 1999.

Rawls, John. *Lectures on the History of Moral Philosophy*, ed. by Barbara Herman. Harvard University Press, 2000.

Rawls, John. *Justice as Fairness: A Restatement*. Harvard University Press, 2001.

Rodrik, Dani. "Why do economists disagree? http://rodrik.typepad.com/dani_rodriks_weblog/2007/08/why-do economis.html (2007, August 5th).

Ross, W.D. *The Foundations of Ethics*, Oxford Clarendon Press, 1939.

Rousseau, Jean-Jacques. *The Social Contract and other Later Political Writings*, ed. and trans. By Victor Gourevitch. Cambridge University Press, 1997.

Rousseau, Jean-Jacques. "Discourse on the Origin of Inequality," in *Classics of Moral and Political Philosophy*, ed, by Steven M. Cahn, Oxford University Press, 2012

Sabl, Andrew. "Looking Forward to Justice: Rawlsian Civil Disobedience and its Non Rawlsian Lessons," *Journal of Political Philosophy* vol. 9, no. 3 (2001): 331-349.

Sandel, Michael. *Liberalism and the Limits of Justice*, Cambridge University Press, 1982.

Sangiovanni, Andrea. "Justice and the Priority of Politics to Morality," *The Journal of Political Philosophy* 16, no. 2 (2008): 137-164.

Scanlon, Thomas. "Contractualism and Utilitarianism," in Amartya Sen and Bernard Williams, *Utilitarianism and Beyond*, Cambridge University Press, 1982: 103–128.

Scheffler, Samuel. *Boundaries and Allegiances*. Oxford University Press, 2001.

Scheffler, Samuel. "Rawls and Utilitarianism," in *The Cambridge Companion to Rawls*, ed. by Samuel Freeman, 2003.

Schmidtz, David. "Nonideal Theory: What it is and What it Needs to be," *Ethics* 121, no. 4 (2011): 772-796.

Sen, Amartya, "Equality of What?" in *Tanner Lectures on Human Values*, ed. by Sterling McMurrin, Cambridge University Press, 1980.

Sen, Amartya. *Poverty and Famines*. Oxford Clarendon Press, 1981.

Sen, Amartya. *Commodities and Capabilities*. Oxford University Press, 1999

Sen, Amartya. *Development as Freedom*. New York: Knopf, 1999.

Sen, Amartya. "What do we want from a Theory of Justice?" *The Journal of Philosophy* 53, no. 5 (2006): 215-238.

Sen, Amartya. *The Idea of Justice*. Harvard University Press, 2009.

Simmons, John A. "Ideal and Nonideal Theory," *Philosophy and Public Affairs* 38, no. 1 (2010): 5-36.

Singer, Peter. "Famine, Affluence and Morality," *Philosophy and Public Affairs* 1, no. 3 (1972): 229-243.

Singer, Peter, *Democracy and Disobedience*, Oxford: Clarendon Press, 1973.

Smith, Adam. *The Theory of Moral Sentiments,* ed. by D.D. Raphael and A.L. Macfie. Oxford University Press, 1976.

Stemplowska, Zofia and Adam Swift. "Ideal and Nonideal Theory" in *The Oxford Handbook of Political Philosophy*, ed. by David Estlund. Oxford University Press, 2012.

Stemplowska, Zofia and Adam Swift. "Rawls on Ideal and Nonideal Theory," in *A Companion to Rawls*, ed. by Jon Mandle and David A. Reidy. Wiley-Blackwell, 2014.

Swift, Adam. "The Value of Philosophy in Nonideal Circumstances," *Social Theory and Practice* 34, no. 3 (2008): 363-387.

Tan, Kok-Chor. "Justice and Personal Pursuits," *The Journal of Philosophy* vol. 101, no. 7 (2004): 331-362.

Tan, Kok-Chor. *Justice, Institutions, and Luck*. Oxford University Press, 2012.

Thomason, Krista "The Moral Value of Envy," *The Southern Journal of Philosophy* 53, 2015: 36-53.

Tomlin, Patrick. "Envy, Facts and Justice: A Critique of the Treatment of Envy in Justice as Fairness," *Res Publica* 14 (2008): 101-116.

Tully, James. *Public Philosophy in a New Key, Two Volumes*. Cambridge: Cambridge University Press, 2008.

Valentini, Laura. "On the Apparent Paradox of Ideal Theory," *The Journal of Political Philosophy* vol. 17, no. 3 (2009): 332-355.

Valentini, Laura. "Ideal vs. Non-ideal Theory: A Conceptual Map," *Philosophy Compass* vol. 7, no. 9 (2012): 654-664.

Vrousalis, Nicholas. *The Political Philosophy of G.A. Cohen: Back to Socialist Basics*. Bloomsbury Academic, 2015.

Wallace, R.J. "Practical Reason," in *the Stanford Encyclopedia of Philosophy*, https://plato.stanford.edu/entries/practical-reason/ (2014, March 26th).

Weisberg, Michael. "Three Kinds of Idealization," *The Journal of Philosophy* vol. 104, no. 12 (2007): 639-659.

Weithman, Paul. *Why Political Liberalism?* Oxford University Press, 2012.

Wiens, David. "Prescribing Institutions without Ideal Theory," *The Journal of Political Philosophy* 20, no. 1 (2012): 45-70.

Wiens, David. "'Going Evaluative' to Save Justice from Feasibility – A Pyrrhic Victory," *Philosophical Quarterly* 64, no. 255 (2014): 301-307.

Wiens, David. "Motivational Limitations on the Demands on Justice," *European Journal of Political Theory* 15, no. 3 (2016): 333-352.

Wikipedia contributors. "Newton's Laws of Motion." *Wikipedia, The Free Encyclopedia.* 12 April 2017 <https://en.wikipedia.org/wiki/Newton%27s_laws_of_motion>.

Williams, Bernard. *In the Beginning Was the Deed: Realism and Moralism in Political Argument.* Princeton University Press, 2005.

CPSIA information can be obtained
at www.ICGtesting.com
Printed in the USA
LVHW080105260323
742527LV00017B/176

9 781805 243687